How to Buy Your First Home

by Diana Brodman Summers
Attorney at Law

SPHINX® PUBLISHING
AN IMPRINT OF SOURCEBOOKS, INC.®
NAPERVILLE, ILLINOIS
www.SphinxLegal.com

First Edition, 2003
Second Printing: August, 2003

Published by: **Sphinx® Publishing, An Imprint of Sourcebooks, Inc.®**

Naperville Office
P.O. Box 4410
Naperville, Illinois 60567-4410
630-961-3900
Fax: 630-961-2168
www.sourcebooks.com
www.SphinxLegal.com

This publication is designed to provide accurate and authoritative information in regard to the subject matter covered. It is sold with the understanding that the publisher is not engaged in rendering legal, accounting, or other professional service. If legal advice or other expert assistance is required, the services of a competent professional person should be sought.

From a Declaration of Principles Jointly Adopted by a Committee of the American Bar Association and a Committee of Publishers and Associations

This product is not a substitute for legal advice.

Disclaimer required by Texas statutes.

Library of Congress Cataloging-in-Publication Data

Summers, Diana Brodman.
   How to buy your first home / by Diana Brodman Summers.-- 1st ed.
      p. cm.
   ISBN 1-57248-328-8 (pbk. : alk. paper)
   1. House buying--United States. 2. Residential real
estate--Purchasing--United States. 3. Mortgage loans--United States.
I. Title.
HD259.S86 2003
643'.12'0973--dc21
                                        2003004573

Printed and bound in the United States of America.

BG Paperback — 10 9 8 7 6 5 4 3 2

Contents

ACKNOWLEDGEMENTS

I want to thank Sourcebooks for the opportunity to pass on my years of experience at real estate to others. The real estate market has been a lifelong hobby for me. There is nothing more intriguing for me than reading real estate ads for those expensive castles or following the tales of preservationists and rehabbers.

I also want to thank my husband, Jim, who has shown an infinite amount of patience with my passion for real estate. He willingly passes me the real estate section from the Sunday paper and tags along when I just have to see the latest open house. Even on our honeymoon, Jim agreed to go through an open house with me, despite the fact that we were 2,000 miles away from home.

Introduction

I was very pleased to be asked to help others take that important step to buy their first home. I have bought and sold nine or ten homes. Some houses were bought just to fix up and re-sell at a profit, and others were my dream house of the moment. I have stayed in my dream houses for as short as three months to the current nineteen years. To everyone who buys this book I hope you will benefit from my experiences and mistakes without the pain of going through them yourself.

A home can be the most important thing in a person's life. It represents stability and safety. It holds our dreams and hopes for the future. Even when friends desert us, and family passes to their just reward, we still have our home to provide us with a sanctuary from the problems of life. People grow attached to their homes; the structure becomes their roots, the mental picture that your mind shows you when someone says the word "home."

My parents, like many of yours, bought only one home in their lifetime. That home became the center of every important family activity, even after all the children left to find homes of their own. This was the place we all returned to at holidays, in crises, and when we wanted to become a kid again. This universal feeling is why to this day buying a home is called "The American Dream."

Once you have made that decision to go with The American Dream, the hardest thing is the waiting to make it come true for you. There is nothing worse than really wanting to own your own home, but thinking that right now you can't even afford to look. For those who are frustrated because home ownership seems years in the future, there are activities that you can start doing today to prepare for this biggest purchase of your life. In fact, the more time you have to prepare for a home purchase the more likely that the purchase will go smoothly and you will get the exact home you want.

The three top things you need to get your own home are:

- patience;
- Internet access; and,
- a willingness to work hard to make your dream come true.

Notice that *a lot of money* is NOT on this list. While money is part of any purchase, it is more important that you have the patience and willingness to research for the right home to meet your budget. In this case, the more information you have, the easier it will be to select a home that you can afford. Remember that you can always sell the house you bought on a budget when your salary increases.

PURPOSE OF THIS BOOK

The purpose of this book is to provide the first-time homebuyer with a few tools to make that experience less traumatic. These tools include an overview of the fundamentals of purchasing a home, generic worksheets to use in finding the right home, and Internet websites where the reader can get more extensive information. It would be an impossible task for one book to list all available information on home buying for every part of the country. Therefore, this book is designed to present a general overview of the buying process and acquaint the first-time home buyer with the fundamentals of the purchasing process.

HOW TO USE THIS BOOK

This book is divided into five sections that correspond to the stages a person goes through in finding the right home. Each section has chapters on individual topics. At the end of the book there is a Glossary with definitions of real estate terms, worksheets to help you along the way, and an appendix of useful information.

You may want to start with a quick overview of the Glossary. (I'll bet that you will be surprised with the number of real estate terms you already know.) Then read the entire book, including those sections that are beyond your stage in a house search. Write in the margins, underline important items, highlight, to make this book your own. When you come across a chapter that references a worksheet, make several copies of the worksheet located at the back of the book. Change the terms on the worksheet to fit your needs. Once you have read through the book, use it as a reference tool for your dream house search — now, and later.

Real Estate Laws

In order to use this book, you need to know a few things about real estate law. The primary thing is that laws vary. Laws and regulations on real estate can be different from state to state, county to county, and even city to city. For example, a long-time, well-known law regarding how real estate agents operate in California, may be the exact opposite in Illinois or Texas.

Even cities and towns have their own real estate regulations. In some states, a *transfer tax fee* is charged by both the state and the city where a home is sold. Some cities require water certificates, the pre-payment of an estimated water bill, or other water and sewer fees as part of the real estate transaction. (In the area that I live, there are state, county, and city laws that govern all real estate transactions and fees that need to be paid to all three entities.)

If you are concerned with the effects of local or state laws on your estate transaction, do some additional research on the

Internet. Local realtors who have their own websites can be a source for local laws, as is your state's and county's website.

This book explains the fundamentals of buying a first home in a generic manner. Because real estate laws and regulations differ by location, your state, county, or city may have a specific law that completely disagrees with the book. However the fundamentals of buying that first home remain the same in every part of the country.

SECTION ONE: PRELIMINARIES

chapter one:
Buying versus Renting

Your friends have asked, your parents have asked, maybe even that person in the mirror has asked—why do you want to buy a home? While the need to own a piece of property seems to be one of those basic things like the need to eat, this chapter will present practical reasons to put down roots.

WORDS

Now would be a good time to review the glossary so that you are familiar with some of the real estate terms used in the preliminary chapters. (See pages 135–151.) Most of the terms are things you have heard before.

Three words we use a lot are *closing, mortgage,* and *foreclosure.* Closing is the activity in which the house is sold. We could also say "at the sale of the house," but most real estate people call this event a closing. Chapter 15 is about the closing.

CLICK ON THIS:

My personal award for the top three Internet sites that provide a variety of information that will help you in buying your first home:
- FIRST PLACE:
  www.ginniemae.gov
- SECOND PLACE:
  www.fanniemae.com
- THIRD PLACE is a three-way tie:
  www.fha.com
  www.interest.com and
  www.msn.com
  (house and home selection)

Mortgage is a type of loan that a bank or other financial institution provides the buyer so that the house can be bought. The buyer makes monthly payments on the mortgage, and after a certain number of years, the mortgage is paid-off.

Foreclosure is when the bank or financial institution (*lender*) takes the house from the buyer because the buyer defaulted (did not pay) on the loan. The lender will file a lawsuit against the buyer if loan payments are not made as promised. A court order, also known as a *judgment*, must be entered against you to finalize the foreclosure. This lawsuit must be filed in the area (*jurisdiction*) where the property is located. (The last chapter in this book covers foreclosures.)

FINANCIAL REASONS

The primary reason to own your own home is—money. The money saved in taxes; the money accumulated as equity; and, the money made when selling the house.

CLICK ON THIS:

For a Buy vs. Rent calculator, go to www.ginniemae.gov. For a calculator to see how much you can save in taxes by buying instead of renting, go to www.freddiemac.com

Equity

When people talk about home ownership, they always mention the word *equity*. Technically, equity is the value of your home above the liens (mortgage and loans) against the property. A *lien* is any loan or mortgage where the house is put up as *collateral*. Basically, the lien documents say "if you do not pay this back, I will take your house."

Example #1:

A couple purchases an $80,000 house. They put $15,000 down and take a mortgage for $65,000. At the point of sale, this couple has $15,000 equity in the home.

Example #2:

Look at that same couple in ten years. The mortgage has been paid down to $50,000 (or is the lien on the home). The house itself has increased in value because of the economy and the improvements that the couple made to the home. Ten years later, the home is worth $150,000. Our couple now has $100,000 of equity in their home. (That $15,000 down payment has increased more than if it were invested in some hot stock.)

So that you do not get the idea that this large increase is always the way it turns out, let's give our example couple some problems.

Example #3:

At that same 10-year mark with the home worth $150,000, our couple drops 50% of their income due to one person losing his job. In order to just make their monthly creditor payments, our couple gets a loan for $50,000 against the value of the house. (This is a lien.) This means that with the mortgage of $50,000 and the new loan of $50,000 the total liens against the house are $100,000. Our couple now only has $50,000 equity in their home. (However, this is still better than most investment plans.)

Equity is the value of the house minus any liens against it. *House value* is determined by upkeep of the home, upgrades made to the home, the neighborhood, and the economy.

Liens against your home are not always mortgages. Sometimes when applying for a loan, the lender will require that you put up your home as *collateral*. Whenever your home becomes collateral, there is a lien against your home. Lenders with liens against a home can force the homeowner into court to settle the debt. In some states, this settlement can mean that the home is sold. The IRS and other governmental bodies can also put a lien against your home for back taxes, unpaid fines, and for court judgments. In addition, a lien can be placed against your property by an "unpaid" private contractor. (In some states this is known as a *mechanic's lien.*)

Tax Advantages

Homeowners are allowed to deduct mortgage interest and property taxes from their annual federal income tax filing. Some states also allow these deductions. In the first years of a mortgage, this is a large amount of money because that is when most interest is paid. If you paid *points* when you signed for the mortgage loan, the points cost may be able to be deducted in that year's income tax.

Passing to heirs

For many of us, owning a home and building equity in it allows us to pass something of value to our children. Most of us do not have vast estates or great wealth and, unless we win the lottery, we never will have a lot to pass to the next generation. In fact, the only thing of real value most people have is the home they live in.

For the majority of people, their home is a provider of equity while they are alive, a place of security for their family, and is the only wealth that they can provide their family at death. The family home becomes the center of gatherings, the place where memories are made, and tangible evidence that we have taken the time and worked hard to provide for the future of our family.

Buying vs. Renting

The usual way of thinking is that it is less expensive to rent than to buy. For some people, this is still true. However, as rents increase and property values increase, buying a home is becoming a real money-saver.

The best way to compare buying versus renting for your particular situation is to go back to the Internet and click on www.ginniemae.gov. This site has a section called "Buy vs. Rent." It contains several tools to compare the advantages and disadvantages of owning versus renting. It also includes a calculator to compare your current rent to the purchase price of a home, an up-to-date buy vs. rent comparison, year-by-year savings comparison, and several other charts which compare the costs of buying and renting.

In general, buying a home gives you the financial plus of equity and tax write-offs. The homeowner can decorate as he or she pleases; is not subject to the landlord's rules on noise; and, does not have to wait for the landlord to fix the property.

On the minus side, in order to buy a home, a person may have to put down a sizeable down payment. There are additional costs such as taxes, insurance, and utilities for homeowners. A homeowner also has the responsibility for fixing and maintaining the property, which is usually included in the cost of rent. If you have an active lifestyle, you may not have the time to keep up with the property maintenance. Paying a lawn care service to maintain the property is yet another cost. However, even with several minuses, owning a home financially comes out on top.

True cost of home ownership

You will read a lot in this book about the costs of home ownership. Know right from the beginning that sometimes you will long for those days when your landlord picked up the bill for these costs. Owning a home means that you will pay for maintenance and repair. Of course you can cut these costs by becoming a do-it-yourselfer. Ownership also means paying property taxes, utility bills, and maybe *Homeowners Association* costs. Some of these costs, such as taxes and Homeowner Association fees, can be estimated before you agree to buy the house and should be in your calculations to determine if you can afford that particular property.

Ask questions about costs before you decide to buy a house. Ask the real estate agent, the sellers, anyone who can help. Also, look at the house with an eye as to what will need repair and/or maintenance. For example, if the house has an in-ground pool, there are associated costs with maintenance of that pool. If the house is in an area with a homeowners association and/or a "gated community," there will likely be a monthly fee that is paid to that association. If the house has an old furnace, leaky faucets, broken windows, and other obvious problems that may need to be fixed immediately, calculate the costs of repairs *before* you offer to buy the house.

You cannot eliminate costs that come along with owning a home, but you can anticipate and be prepared for most costs.

INTANGIBLE REASONS

Status

Let's be honest, owning a home gives a person a certain amount of prestige or status. It is an ego boost to be able to brag to your high school friends, who may still be living with their parents, that you own a home. In a family, siblings usually compete with each other for who has the nicest or biggest home. Even without siblings, some of us will brag about our house to relatives and friends.

> **ATTORNEY TIP:**
>
> Some company benefits offer the employee assistance in finding a mortgage lender. Other companies allow employees time off, with pay, for their house closing. Be sure to ask your employer what benefits they have regarding an employee purchasing a home.

Being a homeowner puts a person in a certain bracket even to employers. It equates to an employee who is stable, who will not do things to jeopardize his or her job because of the obligation of paying the mortgage. Some employers believe that home ownership is so important that they provide their employees with benefits in connection with buying a home.

Privacy and Work Schedules

For those of us who have lived in an apartment while being blessed with work schedules or shifts that are opposite to the regular 9 to 5, we know how difficult it can be to sleep when everyone else is up. During our sleep-time, the upstairs neighbors stomp around in their army boots or practice their bowling techniques. Conversely, during the downstairs neighbor's sleep time, we are up making noise. Guaranteed, no matter how soundproofed the building is, that one day when we dearly need to get to sleep, the next door neighbor is having a party. If this sounds like your life, you are a prime candidate for owning a home.

A real benefit of owning your own home is coming and going when you want. You do not have to tiptoe around for fear of having neighbors pound on your door. You can actually turn up the radio to a hearing level instead of merely whisper quiet.

Recently, a major department store has played a TV commercial of a man and wife in their own home. She is up doing exercises on a treadmill and he asks her why she is exercising at three in the morning. The wife responds that she is exercising "because I can." This commercial could be for homeownership. If you own your own home, you can exercise at 3 a.m. without disturbing neighbors or having the landlord hassle you with complaints.

Homeownership also allows personal privacy. In many rental communities, privacy is sorely lacking. Neighbors watch the times others come and go. Visitors are screened. Even those well-meaning neighbors can become busybodies due to thin walls and close proximity.

Community

Community is both a financial and intangible reason to own your own home. Community is the city, county, and state that may provide financial assistance to homeowners. Community is the neighbors who participate in a block watch to prevent crime. Community is the feeling of putting down roots by making this your home.

The financial aspects of a city, county, and state vary from area to area. In some areas, senior citizen homeowners are given financial breaks in property tax and financial assistance. Local cities may provide lawn care or snow shoveling for low or no fees to those who are disabled or on fixed incomes. Some

CLICK ON THIS:

Go to www.ginniemae.gov in the section Homeownership 101. Select "Are you ready to buy?" This is an online calculator that will help review your income, savings, expenses, and debt responsibilities. Use this site now and throughout the rest of this book.

areas also provide low cost professional services such as tax preparation and medical assistance for fixed income homeowners.

As job losses are on the increase, many communities are providing some financial assistance for homeowners in need. This can be in the way of foodstamps, utility discounts, free food pantry, property tax assistance, and other financial benefits to keep the homeowner from losing his or her house to foreclosure.

The intangibles of living in a community are much harder to define. Neighbors can become best friends, especially when their children grow up together. Local churches provide another aspect of membership and additional sources for friendship. Some towns come together to build homes for the disadvantaged or to help some other worthy cause. The intangible of a community is the feeling of belonging with those of like minds. While this feeling could happen in a rental community—those things that are positive in renting—easier to move and no responsibility for property upkeep—stifle this.

Conclusion

So now you are excited. You really want to buy a home, but you are a little concerned. Owning a home doesn't seem so scary, but the act of buying a home means dealing with the frightening unknown (the sellers, the agents, the brokers, the insurance agents, and the lawyers).

Relax and keep reading. By the time you reach the last chapter of this book, you will know what to expect and as a result, buying a home will become a less confusing experience.

chapter two:
Qualifying Yourself for a Mortgage

The reason this is one of the first chapters, is that it is something that should be started before you actually go out and look at houses on the market. Unless you are one of the lucky few people who has enough funds to pay cash for your home, your ability to purchase the home of your dreams depends on your ability to qualify for a sizeable loan—a *mortgage*.

YOUR CREDIT HISTORY

When do you start financially qualifying yourself for a mortgage? When you took out that very first credit card, your student loans, or co-signed for someone else's purchase. Anything that deals with loans, credit, or savings is part of your financial history. Your financial history is a primary piece used by lenders in deciding to issue a mortgage.

Your credit history is captured in a *credit report*. Every lender uses credit reports to qualify a person. Your credit report will show all debts (credit card, loans, mortgages), *payment history* (including late

ATTORNEY TIP:

Three things to do to improve your credit history today:

- make all payments ON TIME;
- pay an extra $20 toward each charge card payment this month; and,
- don't apply for any new charge accounts.

payment instances), amounts currently owed to each creditor, tax liens, bankruptcies, foreclosures, judgments against you, and other public records which would have an impact on a person's financial history.

There are currently three private credit bureaus that electronically keep credit reports:

EQUIFAX:

> Credit Information Services
> PO Box 740256
> Atlanta, GA 30374-0256
> 800-685-1111
> www.equifax.com

EXPERIAN:

> National Consumer Assistance Center
> PO Box 2104
> Allen, TX 75013-2104
> 888-397-3742
> www.experian.com

TRANS UNION:

> National Disclosure Center
> PO Box 1000
> Chester, PA 19022
> 800-888-4213
> www.tuc.com

Each of these credit bureaus has a facility to provide you with your credit report, for a fee. If you have been denied a job, insurance, or credit because of a negative credit report within the past sixty (60) days, you are entitled to receive a *free* credit report upon request.

Some financial experts suggest that everyone annually get a copy of their own credit report from each of these bureaus. This will alert a person to any fraudulent use of their identity or errors in their credit report.

It is very important that you obtain a copy of your own credit report and review it for errors long *BEFORE* applying for a mortgage. If you find errors in your credit report, contact the credit bureau. Each credit bureau has its own procedures for correcting errors. These procedures can take considerable time. Once you discover an error on your credit report in one credit bureau, it is probable that this error will be reflected in the reports at the other two bureaus.

Besides errors, your credit report may show a history of late payments and the amount of outstanding debt that you currently have. While a history of late payments won't totally

---

ATTORNEY TIP:

Reduce your credit card debt starting today. Try to pay extra on each monthly payment. Tape a picture of a house you like on your wallet so that each time you reach for that credit card, the picture reminds you what you are saving for.

---

disqualify you from obtaining a mortgage, it may cause the lender to charge you a higher rate of interest. By reviewing your credit report long before you are ready to get a mortgage, you give yourself time to correct things such as a history of late payments and the pay-off of outstanding bills.

CREDIT SCORES

A *credit score* is a number computed by the private credit bureaus to indicate the likelihood that a person will pay his or her bills on time. Each credit bureau calculates its own range of scores, so you would probably have three different scores. This score is sometimes referred to as an *FICO score*, because Fair Isaac & Co developed it.

FICO scores take into account a person's credit history. Such things as late payment, amount of credit available, amount of credit used, length of time in a job, length of time living in a location, bankruptcy, and all other financial items are used to calculate this score. FICO scores should not take into account a

CLICK ON THIS:

Choose either of the following sites to get a more detailed explanation of FICO scores and ways to put your FICO in an acceptable range:

www.yourmortgage.net

www.myfico.com

person's race, religion, national origin, sex, or marital status.

Some mortgage lenders will base the decision to give a person a mortgage loan almost totally on this number. However, FICO is not the only factor that most mortgage lenders use. As with other factors on your credit report, in order to keep your FICO score in an acceptable range pay bills on time, use credit sparingly, and reduce credit card balances.

CREDIT REPORT ERRORS

When is a credit report error not really an error? The answer is when the item on the credit report is there because of a misunderstanding.

Example #1

Bob and Jeff are brothers. Bob is going to college and has very little money. Jeff lives near and has held a paying job for years. Bob needs a 'beater' car to drive to classes. He found a great deal at URRIPOFF car dealer, but needs someone who has a job to co-sign for the loan. Jeff, being a good brother, offers to co-sign.

Within months, the car won't run and is abandoned in the school parking lot. Bob drops out of school and is now touring with the rock band "The Purple Drums."

Jeff applies for a mortgage, but is turned down because of a legal judgement on his credit report. That judgement was because URRIPOFF car dealer was never paid for Bob's car. Since Jeff co-signed for the loan, Jeff is legally liable.

Example #2

Suzie had a car accident. She totaled both her car and the one she hit. At the accident scene Suzie was given two tickets and told the accident was her fault. Suzie turned everything over to her insurance company and forgot about the accident.

Later that year, Suzie changed her name to Suzanna Sunshine and moved to Hollywood to be a star. After a few years, she applied for a mortgage and was turned down because of a legal judgement placed against her. Suzie's legal judgement was from the other driver who sued her and the insurance company. Because Suzie could not be located, she was not able to defend herself in court and the judgement was placed on her credit history.

These are just two examples of unexpected things that may appear on a person's credit report. In the first example Jeff thought that Bob would make the payments on the car and thought nothing more about it. In the second, Suzie figured the insurance company would handle the problem. Had Jeff and Suzie gotten their credit report before they applied for a mortgage, they would have had time to repair the credit report.

Not all financial problems on a person's credit report are because of misunderstandings. Real errors can include a mix up with people of the same name, identity theft, bills for items not received, creditors who promise to reduce or cancel a debt but do not, and computer input errors.

Example:

David is a car enthusiast. He is restoring a collection of 1970's Porsches. David spent $2,500 for a fancy fuel injector system from Puddles Porsche. Unfortunately, the system was defective. David stopped payment on his $2,500 check and wants to return the product.

Puddles believes that David broke the system when he attempted to install it on his Chevy Nova. Puddles will not accept the return. After much arguing over the phone, Mrs. Puddles finally tells David to just return the item and the debt will be forgotten.

Nothing was put in writing. Years later, David finds out that Puddles brought legal action against him for the $2,500, which is now a blemish on his credit report.

ATTORNEY TIP:

Two important things to remember when dealing with any Credit Bureau:

1). BE COURTEOUS.

No matter how big the problem is or how much it is affecting your life, keep your composure. The people at the credit bureau are employees too. They probably did not cause the problem and they can be invaluable in correcting it.

2). DOCUMENT IN WRITING.

Write down whom you spoke to, the date, the time, and what was decided. If you are attempting to repair a problem, send a letter to that person reminding her or him what was said, what needs to be done, and when the agreed action was to take place.

REPAIRING YOUR CREDIT REPORTS

Once you get your credit report, what happens if it has errors? Understand that each credit reporting bureau has its own procedures for correcting error. You MUST follow their instructions to correct error, no matter how dumb the instructions sound.

In general, the following will help you deal with the errors on your credit report.

What is the error? Is this a loan you co-signed for? Is this a bill you forgot to pay? Is this something you never heard of? You need to do some detective work *BEFORE* you fix the error.

If you co-signed for a car loan, contact the person you signed for. If the error is an item bought from a store you never went to, call the store. Get copies of receipts for things you supposedly bought.

If the error is for something you returned or a debt that you were told was cancelled, find your documentation on that debt.

If you are lucky enough to have physical proof that a debt was resolved (cancelled check or other document) let the credit bureau know. If they ask you to send a copy of the document, include a letter saying what the copy is and how it effects the item on your credit report (even if you have already told the credit bureau several times). Remember that the spoken word is usually not enough to resolve a credit bureau error. It must be written down and signed.

CLICK ON THIS:

The Federal Trade Commission (FTC) website is www.ftc.gov. This site has helpful information for home buyers in both English and Spanish.

State and federal laws regulate credit reporting agencies and procedures. The *Federal Trade Commission (FTC)* is the government agency that monitors credit bureaus.

You have the right to correct items on your credit report. The FTC website provides the information you need to remove false information from your file. Contact the credit bureau for the necessary steps. You can also place your own brief explanation of negative information in your credit file if the bureau investigates and stands by the negative information.

If the error involves a court judgment you may need to hire an attorney to research and resolve this.

ATTORNEY TIP:

If you determine that a reporting error has occurred on your credit report, do not pay a credit repair agency to correct it. You can do this for free.

chapter three:
Calculating What You Can Afford

Every lender has a formula to tell how much a person can afford in mortgage payments. Formulas are good because they can give a definitive number. However, most formulas do not factor in a person's lifestyle (what is important to that person), future financial down-turns, or what each person feels comfortable paying for housing.

TOTAL DEBT-TO-INCOME RATIO

Many lenders depend on a calculation of a person's total debt to their total monthly income. The income is *gross monthly* or what is received each month from every source before taxes and before deductions for employer incentive savings program (401k). This amount is multiplied by a rate. The rate varies from lender to lender. What results is the approximate amount the person can pay for a monthly mortgage payment.

Currently, a lot of lenders are using a rate of 0.36 to 0.41. (This could change by the time you are reading this section.)

CLICK ON THIS:

Use the "Affordability Calculator" at www.ginniemae.gov. This allows you to enter your income amount and the amount of your debt to get an estimate of how much house you can afford.

The actual calculation, however, is relatively simple.

Say your gross monthly income is $5,000
The lender's ratio is 0.36
$5,000.00 x 0.36 = $1,800.00

This means that your monthly expenses such as credit card payments, student loan payments, utilities, food, insurance, alimony, child support, and the mortgage cannot exceed $1,800 each month.

If the same person is trying to get a loan that uses the ratio of 0.41 the calculation is:

$5,000.00 x 0.41 = $2,050.00

HOUSING DEBT-TO-INCOME RATIO

Another calculation which some lenders use to determine how much a person can afford is what we're commonly told even for renting—housing should be no more than one quarter of your monthly gross income. Currently, lenders range from using ratios of 0.25 to 0.28. The dollar income amount is still a gross amount (that is, before taxes and employer deductions).

CLICK ON THIS:

Choose the Debt to Income Ratios path on www.fha.com to get examples of these calculations and how lenders use them.

Using the example above, we can calculate how much this person can pay for just the monthly mortgage payments using the housing *debt-to-income ratio* the calculation is:

$5,000.00 x 0.25 = $1,250.00
or
$5,000.00 x 0.28 = $1,400.00

Using this formula, our future homeowner can pay somewhere within a range of $1250 to $1400 for a monthly mortgage *or* a total for expenses between $1,800 to $2,050.

FROM MONTHLY PAYMENT TO TOTAL MORTGAGE

Homes are not sold by quotes of monthly payments. They have total prices. While knowing what your lender expects your ratio to be is important, in reality, it is how the *total price* of the home computes into monthly payments that means more when looking for a home.

For example, if the ratio comes up that you can afford a monthly mortgage payment of $1,000 that really means that with a mortgage of 6% interest, the total price of the house you can purchase is around $165,000. If the mortgage is at 7% interest that total purchase price drops to around $150,000.

This total purchase price is after your down payment is subtracted. If you can put $10,000 down on a home, you should be looking at homes with a price no greater than $160,000 or $175,000.

ADDITIONAL CHARGES INCLUDED IN THE MORTGAGE PAYMENT

Although the ratios calculate what a person can afford in a monthly mortgage payment in black and white, this calculation is for a payment that is only made up of the *principal* and *interest* amount. Mortgage payments always include other amounts. These other amounts can substantially increase the

CLICK ON THIS:

Choose any of the following sites to check for mortgage calculations:

www.interest.com

www.fha.com

www.mortgageselect.com

www.ginniemae.gov

www.hud.gov

www.freddiemac.com

www.hgtv.com

total dollar amount of the payments. Besides paying interest and principal on a loan, the mortgage payment usually includes real estate or *property taxes*, homeowners insurance, and/or *mortgage insurance*.

Besides getting a loan at the lowest amount and putting up a down payment which is as large as possible, the new home owner must be concerned with the taxes of the neighborhood and the cost of insurance.

YOUR LIFESTYLE

Up to this point we have been concerned with the routine ratios that lenders use, but that is not all that you should consider in determining how much you can afford to pay every month for that mortgage. Living in your own home is more than just mortgage payments. Just for the home there is upkeep, furniture, decorating, inevitable breakdowns, and utility bills. Buying your perfect home, but being unable to afford any furniture or to keep the heat at a comfortable level must also be considered.

Ratios do not know how you and your family want to live. Are vacations important? Do you anticipate college expenses? Do you want to buy a new car every couple of years? These factors are part of your lifestyle and you should not be forced to compromise a lifestyle for a piece of property.

Another issue to consider is emergencies. If the amount of mortgage payment plus other debts leaves little or no money for savings in case of an emergency, you are cutting things too close. In our current economy, downsizing, job loss, and wage cuts have become a reality, and everyone needs to prepare for the worst.

> **ATTORNEY TIP:**
>
> I always use the ratio calculation from the lender as the <u>maximum</u> top end that I will pay on a mortgage. I take their total number and then deduct 20% to come up with a comfortable mortgage payment amount. This translates into buying less of a home than I want, but having a cushion for emergencies, new cars, and living. I can always add improvements to my home as time goes on.

What a person can afford to pay in monthly mortgage payments is a personal amount. This amount cannot be just a cold calculation, but must take into count how you live and what you want to do with your life. Despite what some lenders claim, it is no longer a guarantee that people's income will increase as time goes on.

chapter four:
Qualifying the Neighborhood

You have probably heard the old real estate joke—what are the top three things that make a house sell? Location, location, location! This is not just a joke. In reality, when you buy a home you are not just buying a building, you are buying a neighborhood. A good neighborhood is one where homes increase in value. And while being concerned with the *re-sale value* of your dream house before you even buy it may seem silly, it is that re-sale value that will determine if you can get the money back you invested in your home when you do sell. It is that re-sale value that allows you to *re-finance* at a lower rate, and even get a loan against the value of your home if you need a large amount of cash. The re-sale value proves that your choice of a home was a good investment.

HOW TO RESEARCH A NEIGHBORHOOD

On the Internet

To find a good neighborhood you will need to go through lots of numbers such as crime statistics, school ratings, and demographic information. Almost all of these numbers are readily available by doing searches on the Internet. One great site is **www.msn.com** in the section called "House and Home." From that site you can search for the right neighborhood by your personal criteria.

Many cities and counties have their own web sites. Some local Chambers of Commerce or other organizations also have websites. Begin by looking up the city and state on your favorite search engine (my personal favorite is **www.google.com**). The results may surprise you.

Many real estate professionals are putting up web sites that contain current homes for sale in an area. Some of these sites are so automated that they contain walking tours of the inside of the house. Most give the reader generalized help in buying a home in addition to the sales pitch. This is a great way to view a home without leaving the comfort of your computer. It is also a way to select a knowledgeable real estate agent or one who concentrates on finding the type of property/mortgage you want.

Field Trips

Field trips are great ways to get information about an area. Find the town's main business district and take a walk. Pick up the local newspapers and flyers. While you are on foot, stop by the local *Welcome Wagon* and *Chamber of Commerce*, to see if they have information on the town.

Besides walking, you should try to drive through the area at rush hour. Calculate how long it will take you to get from this new area to your current job. Look at traffic patterns. Is rush hour a noisy mess with bumper to bumper traffic and public transportation on some streets? Does that make certain streets and driveways almost non-accessible because you can't make a left turn in the rush hour?

If you live in an area where you are blessed(?) with snow, check to see how the streets are cleared. Does the town spread salt or other ice reducers? Are the streets clean and swept? Are streets in good repair or are you dodging potholes? Besides upkeep, look for abandoned buildings, undesirables, graffiti, gang marks, trash, and signs that the city is not keeping up with trash collection. Some home appraisers look at areas that have a lot of rental properties as not being as desirable. The reason is that most transient people do not keep the property up, as would the property owners.

Once you are close to picking a home, walk the blocks around the home you are considering. Talk to neighbors; check it out at various times of the day and night, weekday and weekends. Check traffic patterns. Remember, a yellow line down the middle of a street is a good indicator of high traffic volume. Check out the parking. Is there enough for both residents and guests. Check out the next door property. Is it well maintained? Are there broken and abandoned vehicles on the property?

Don't expect to figure this out in one field trip. Visit your new town often.

On another field trip, visit the village or town hall. Tell them you are interested in the area. You may even be able to get written reports about the property values, restrictions on changing property, and building codes. You can learn a lot about how local government treats the taxpayers by this visit. If you are looking at a big city, the challenge is finding aldermen, local representatives, or others who will actually admit to being part of the government.

In the Library

Many cities and towns have their own library. This is a wealth of information about the area, in addition to being a good field trip for your research. Just thumbing through the local phone book will give you an idea of the availability of doctors, veterinarians, dentists, grocery stores, real estate professionals, etc.

Some libraries may have a history of the town to read. This is usually a place to find those all-important demographics about crime, schools, and property values. Some of the nicest people work at local libraries; many of them are lifelong residents who are anxious to share their knowledge.

Besides libraries, some towns have Historic Preservation Offices, museums, and other local offices that promote the town.

From Your Couch

The greatest tool you can use to learn about real estate in general is to read the real estate section in the newspaper. Big cities (like Chicago) produce large real estate sections weekly or more often, that contain real estate ads, articles, and items of interest to homeowners. Even if you are not looking for a home in the big city, these papers are invaluable. The articles alone are worth the price of the paper, plus, reading real estate ads will prepare you for what you want in your own home. If you see that many homes are now advertising central air conditioning, and that increases the value of the home, you may decide to put central air on your must have list.

This is also a great way to determine if you can afford to live in a particular town. If all the homes advertised are going for double or triple what you can afford, you may need to rethink that town. On the other hand, if you are set on that expensive area, you may have to compromise in the size, condition, or features of a house.

Besides the larger newspapers, the town or city you are interested in may have its own newspaper. These can be great for researching the benefits of living in that city. They usually have local real estate ads and may even list the actual selling price of property after the deal is done. Once you decide what town you want to live in, it is worth the price of having their local newspaper delivered. Of course, this does not mean that a paperboy will bike miles from home to get you this out of town newspaper. Most out-of-town subscriptions are sent through the mail. You may miss some last minute local sales, but you will learn a lot about the neighborhood. Many newspapers are even available on the Internet.

Another paper listing that you will want to read are the flyers or magazines that list homes for sale. In many towns, they are placed at the entrance of local grocery stores, at community centers, at train stations, and at real estate offices. The contents usually are made up of ads of homes for sale complete with picture, description, and often, asking price.

HOW TO SELECT A LOCATION

What it all boils down to is what is important to you and your lifestyle. Remember you want to purchase a home that will increase in re-sale value. For that alone you should avoid high crime areas, areas where there are many abandoned buildings, and areas where the city services are scarce or non-existent.

For many people, the length of time it takes to commute to their job will determine where they will live. Some start with a map of the area and calculate how long it takes to get to work from different points. (However, with our economy of lessening job security and companies moving to cheaper areas this may backfire.)

Recent economic studies have shown that the cost of transportation between home and job is rising faster than the cost of a mortgage payment. Higher gas prices, higher costs for public transportation, and the significant population increase in suburbs farther away from large cities are to blame.

Example #1:

David Doodzie loved to drive his bright, safety-orange Porsche to work, but he didn't want to spend more than 45 minutes on the freeway even in bad weather. As an experiment, once a week, David drove to work at the normal time, but took a different freeway and would drive for 45 minutes then exit. After a while, David was able to plot on a map the farthest extent of where he would want to live and he became familiar with the housing choices closest to the off ramps.

Example #2:

David's sister Octavia hated to drive or ride in David's Porsche. She wanted to be near public transportation. Octavia also did not want to limit herself to the company she had been working for which was in a suburb of a medium size city. By doing research on the public transportation available in that area, Octavia found two means of public transportation (bus and train line) that supported both the suburb where she was currently working and the medium size city that had more jobs. She started taking short trips after work on both the bus and train line to learn more about the neighborhoods they served.

You and your family need to decide what is important to you in a neighborhood. Do you need to be in a certain school system, close to an elderly family member, close to other family members, within walking distance to favorite recreational locations?

You should not compromise on schools. The re-sale value of a home has a connection to the schools in the area. The majority of property tax usually goes towards the local school. In an area where schools must be upgraded to meet state and national guidelines, it is almost a guarantee that property taxes will increase. Many people, even those without children, judge a neighborhood on the quality of the schools.

Before you decide what is important, ask everyone in your family (especially your spouse) what are the top five things they want in a neighborhood. Then compare lists. Worksheet 1 in Appendix D on page 168 will help you in this decision.

THE FOOD SHOPPING TEST

Once the excitement of getting your first home wears off, the reality of having to live in that neighborhood sets in. Along with day-to-day living comes the usual chores that everyone does. For most of us, weekly food shopping can be one of the most boring and one of the most expensive chores.

While I would like to take credit for this particular test of the neighborhood, I must admit that my husband, Jim, developed this test when we were looking for our first home. We had narrowed the search down to a few different areas in Chicago and its suburbs. He based this test on the fact that living expenses vary from area to area, from suburb to suburb, especially in big cities like Chicago.

The test is simple. Take your regular grocery shopping list and shop at what would be your choice of grocery stores in the new neighborhood. Try to purchase all the items that you would normally get, and make note of the prices for those special items that you buy once in a while. Then compare the prices to what you usually spend or to other neighborhoods under consideration.

When we did the food-shopping test we were able to eliminate two areas because the *cost of living*, just for the weekly food bill, was at least 15% higher than what we had budgeted. Other things that we learned doing this test was that some areas had a limited selection of grocery stores or those that carried what we wanted were a long drive away.

While doing this test, we also ran into stores that had security gates, bars on the windows, barriers from taking the grocery cart to the parking lot, and other high security measures. We decided that if the local business owners felt the neighborhood was so unsafe, it was not the area for us. This did however, eliminate our moving into an area where we could both walk to work and walk to a great city nightlife. These are the type of decisions and trade offs that must be made when looking for an area to live.

> **ATTORNEY TIP:**
>
> Remember to pick up any area flyers that appear in the entrance of many grocery stores. In some areas, the flyer that contains homes for sale extends up to fifty pages or more.

OTHER COST OF LIVING AMOUNTS

In addition to groceries, you may wish to check with your automobile insurance agent to see if your rates will change depending upon the area. In some neighborhoods, the large amount of auto thefts and damage will cause higher rates. Most insurance agents will be happy to advise you on this.

While you are talking to your insurance agent, you should ask for an estimate of homeowners insurance. Like auto insurance, the neighborhood can cause high rates. In addition, some insurance companies will discount premiums when a person purchases multiple types of policies from one provider.

Again, remember transportation costs. If you drive to work, this is the cost of wear, repairs, and gas in your car, plus the costs of tolls and parking. If you take public transportation, it is your ticket price. Since transportation costs are increasing for across the country, this is an important expense. If you plan to take public transportation, your calculation is as easy as getting the ticket price.

If you drive to work, calculating your costs is more difficult. Begin with monthly car payments, cost of gas (need to know the miles per gallon of gas that your car gets), tolls or highway fees, cost of parking, and wear cost. For wear, take a guess at the cost of repairs that driving daily will cause. Older cars may not take the daily commute, so you may need to figure in the cost of buying a new car.

Another transportation cost that is rarely spoken of is the cost of your wasted time. Most of us have heard that old saying time is money. No place is that truer than in the daily commute. If your dream home requires a one hour commute to your job and a one hour commute back, that calculates to ten hours a week or over twenty days a year. This can be a real waste of your time.

Public transportation may allow you to spend that commuting time dutifully working on your laptop computer, but public transportation puts you at the mercy of someone else's schedule.

Weigh these factors carefully when looking for the right neighborhood. Don't just look at the dollars and cents of commuting, look at how you will feel about that long commute after the excitement of buying your home.

PUBLIC IMPROVEMENT PLANS

Investigate local real estate issues. Is a road about to be widened in your desired neighborhood? Your property value could be reduced. Worse yet, your house could be condemned and purchased at a reduced price by local government if it is in the path of the proposed road. This process is called *eminent domain*.

Eminent domain is invoked when a government unit wants to make a public improvement such as building a new airport, expanding an existing airport, public school, college, or hospital.

In many states, the seller and his realtor have a duty to reveal any public improvements when known. Some states require that the seller and his realtor reveal this information only if you specifically ask. For your protection, always submit the question in writing and insist on a written answer.

> **ATTORNEY TIP:**
>
> Read the local newspapers in order to be alerted to any public improvement plans in the area you are searching.

OLD vs. NEW

Neighborhoods can generally be classified as either old or new. There are benefits and liabilities in both types. In a new area, the homes are usually modern with the latest extras. You may even be able to select options before the home is built. New areas usually attract younger people and those who are beginning their family.

On the down side, a new area has not established its tax base, so you can expect property tax increases. Property owners may also be charged with assessments to install sidewalks, widen streets, install traffic controls, install sewer system, etc. The mostly younger population may mean lots of children, who will need additional schools to be built, which increases property taxes. If the neighborhood is being built as you move in, there is construction noise, dust, and debris. There is also the additional cost of landscaping that must be considered.

An older, established neighborhood has probably put in the sidewalks, sewers, and streets. However, this is no guarantee that these items will not need replacement and increase taxes through a special assessment. The other pluses of an older neighborhood are that homes are relatively stable in construction and taxes are consistent. (However, taxes may rise if there is a lot of tear-down activity.)

An older neighborhood also has negatives. Some home-owners become complacent or become physically unable to keep up their property and houses can suffer from disrepair. City services may go down because the stable tax revenue is not keeping up with the increasing costs for city workers and sup-plies. An older neighborhood can also become victim to the construction traffic when homes are sold, leveled, and replaced with a very expensive structure.

SECTION TWO: SEARCHING FOR YOUR HOME

chapter five:
Deciding which House Features are Important

Before you begin the actual search for your home, you must decide what you would *like* to have and what you really *need*. This is a serious decision that takes into account those things absolutely necessary plus the reality of having to pay for your house.

THE BUILDING, ITSELF

This is not going to be a book on exterior home designs. There are many books and magazines that cover that subject. You should be able to tell the difference between a ranch style and a bungalow, but may not want to distinguish an American foursquare from a Victorian.

In order to learn what these terms mean in your area, read the real estate ads that have pictures. Review classic "House" magazines that show interesting homes.

> **ATTORNEY TIP:**
>
> Best way to learn about real estate in general and in a particular area is to read the real estate section of the local newspaper every time it is available. You will become familiar with common real estate terms and learn the types and prices of homes that are available in the area.

You may also want to start a file for articles and pictures of homes and/or decorating ideas that interest you. Review this file often. Add to it frequently. Keep it current and you will begin to see what home design most appeals to you.

Besides the design, you should be concerned with what is on the outside of the structure. If the home is brick, it is strong, but may be expensive to add a room on to the house. It may be drafty without proper insulation. If the home is covered in stucco, the finish should last a long time, but when a repair is required, it may be difficult to match the existing stucco. If the home is done in aluminum/vinyl siding, it is close to maintenance free, but you will not be able to change the color. If you add a room to the house you may not be able to match the siding. If the home is wood siding, you can change the color, but depending on what the siding is painted with, you may have to re-paint or re-stain the house annually.

There are new options for the exterior of a home coming out every year. Be sure you know both the positives and negatives for any exterior covering on the home you are considering purchasing.

FEATURES

The *features* or the *interior layout* and amenities of a home are usually what a person is mainly concerned with. Do you dream of a winding staircase that your children will scramble down on Christmas morning? Do you dream of a private bath in the master bedroom suite for relaxing after a hard day? Do you need a handicapped accessible kitchen or a home with ramps? How much property or lawn do you want?

You need to decide what you want in a home; how important each feature is to you; and what is absolutely necessary. This is the time to be realistic. If you always wanted an indoor pool, but can barely afford more than two bedrooms, save that pool dream for a future home. There is nothing to stop a person from buying a home with more features in the future, as their income increases.

To help you with this decision I have supplied Worksheet 2 in Appendix D on page 167 to prioritize the features you want and which ones you will compromise on. Make lots of copies of this worksheet. As time goes by and you start looking at homes for sale, you will be changing your mind, often. If you are planning to buy a home with another person, make him or her fill one of these forms out and then compare what both parties want in a home. An interesting exercise is to save your final list after you have bought your home. Pull it out in a few years and see if you still feel the same.

ESSENTIALS

Essentials is another word for features, but these are the features that you absolutely MUST have. A lot of essentials vary from area to area. For example, in Southern California, an in-ground pool is an essential (in my mind). In Chicago, an in-ground pool, unless it has a building around it, will cause the home to decrease in value.

Most areas have their own essentials: air conditioning in Las Vegas, heated garage in Minnesota, and so on. Learn about the area to determine what are essentials. If you are moving in from another state, look at the real estate ads to see what features are advertised as part of the homes for sale. What is an essential feature in one state, may be a major problem in another.

As with anything else with your home, you must decide what is important to you, and then determine if that will work in the area you want to live.

HANDY-MAN'S SPECIAL & FIXER-UPPER

If you have been reading the real estate ads you will see these two terms. The real estate industry has no set definition for what constitutes a *handy-man's special* or a *fixer-upper*. It depends a lot on the area of the country and what the seller thinks can actually be fixed. In reality, these structures range from "an amateur can fix" to "must hire professional contractors" to "should be leveled."

The price on one of these homes can be much less than the surrounding area. If you have decided that the neighborhood you want to live in is generally above your price range, this may be one way that you can get into that neighborhood. But realize that this type of home takes a lot of work and you will either have to do it yourself or have to pay someone to do the work. The big question is the quality of the structure of the house. If the structure is poor then renovations will be more expensive.

If you are like me and picked the old stately neighborhood with large older homes, you may already be preparing to *rehab* your home. Be sure that you know what you are getting into. Do-it-yourself remodeling requires an infinite amount of patience with construction rubble, a large amount of time and commitment, and the physical ability to do the work.

ATTORNEY TIP:

Rule of thumb when doing home repairs: it will take three times longer and cost three times more than what you originally estimated. Be prepared.

Several years ago there was a movie, "The Money Pit," about problems and expenses in rehabbing a home. While some of the things that happened to these fictional characters were a bit extreme, (the characters seem to have an unlimited amount of money), the movie is worth seeing for any potential rehabber.

Before you decide to look for a "needs work" home, honestly asses your abilities to do the work. Take a field trip to one of your local home repair superstores. That will give you some idea of the expenses that even do-it-yourselfers face. Many of the home repair superstores provide free classes and literature on do-it-yourself projects.

As I have mentioned throughout this book, I chose a "needs work" Victorian home in a perfect suburb. My husband, Jim, assured me that he was able to do the repairs since he and his dad had built a family room in his parent's home. However, after we had moved in my mother-in-law told me that my husband's help consisted of going for lunch and passing tools.

The bottom line is that you need to really know your limitations and be willing to learn new trades. Maybe you cannot rewire the house, but you might be a wizard at putting up wallpaper. Over the years Jim has even surprised himself at what he has been able to do. However, he has also learned when to call a professional.

WE ARE ALL GETTING OLDER

As uncomfortable as it may be, we are all aging and so are our families. We all get to that time of our life when health or age dictates that we either stay in our home or go to a place where someone will take care of us. You may have to make that decision for you parents or other relatives. While this may be the farthest thought from your mind when looking at your first home, you may want to take a moment to consider the future.

Houses where all the bedrooms are on the second floor are great—until you break your foot or become sick or are too weak to go up and down the stairs. The same is true for homes that have steep stairs at the entrance without the room to install ramps for handicapped access. A home needs to bend and accommodate you and your family in the future. Take a minute to assess the potential that in a few years elderly parents or relatives may have to move in with you.

Now I do not advocate buying a huge house on the chance that Grandma Millie or Uncle Pete will move in. However, if there is someone in the family who may be in that situation, it is better to find a home that will accommodate the future changes without complete disruption of your life.

chapter six:
Working with Real Estate Agents and Brokers

Once you pick out the neighborhood and are really ready to buy a home, you will probably select a real estate agent. The best place to look for your agent is in the neighborhood you want to buy in. The local agent is probably where the current owners will go to sell their property. Local agents also have the advantage of knowing a lot about the community.

REAL ESTATE PROFESSIONALS

The term *real estate professionals* usually refers to *real estate agents* and *real estate brokers*. The primary function of agents and brokers is to assist buyers and sellers in the legal transaction of transferring property from one person to another. Because this is a legal function with great implications on the public, agents and brokers are state licensed. Each state has its own requirements to obtain these licenses. Most require education in real estate, a term of working in the area of real estate, and continuing education.

Appendix A lists the department in each state that controls the licensing of real estate professionals, and their particular Internet site. Many states have Internet sites that provide consumer information about licensed agents/brokers and how to utilize these professionals in buying a home.

Real estate agents work independently (sometimes out of their home), as an employee for a well-known real estate agency, or, even for a large corporation as relocation specialists. No matter what type of office the agent has, it is their experience and commitment to the profession that is important.

The Real Estate Profession

The reality of the real estate profession is that it is plagued with high turnover. This means that many of the real estate agents are relative newcomers. While there is nothing wrong with a newcomer to a job, when someone is helping me with the largest purchase of my life I want a person who has been on the job at least two years in that area.

This profession also attracts the part time or retired worker who does not want to or cannot work an eight-hour day. Again, that does not make the person incompetent, however in a purchase this large I want to know that my real estate agent is available to return my calls and look at new listings.

Because this type of work is dealing with almost daily changes in listings, real estate law, mortgage rules, and financing, it is important that the real estate agent has made the time commitment to keep up with his or her job.

An agent who views this as his or her only job, not a hobby or extra moneymaker, is able to bring professionalism and commitment to the transaction. He or she wants to keep you as a happy customer because they know that if you are satisfied you will recommend him or her to your friends and family. Most people move several times in their lives. A happy customer can be a source of continued revenue for this agent.

One indicator of commitment is a real estate agent's taking advanced educational courses that provide training in all aspects of the real estate trans-

ATTORNEY TIP:

When choosing a real estate agent, look for one who is as committed to his or her job as you have been to finding a home. Look for someone who is knowledgeable, available, and able to work for the commission.

action. The *National Association of REALTORS®* offers nationwide programs. This organization awards a designation of a GRI to those who have passed the *REALTORS® Graduate* series of courses. Real estate agents who have completed advanced courses use it as a tool for marketing and display such designations on business cards, ads, and at their desk.

PROBLEMS WITH REAL ESTATE AGENTS

Unfortunately, there are real estate agents that conduct themselves as surrogate mothers for their clients. They are so sure that they know exactly what the clients want now and for the future, that they tend to turn a deaf ear to what the potential buyers are actually saying that they want.

> ## CLICK ON THIS:
>
> The National Association of Realtors has a great web site to help find a home:
>
> www.realtor.com
>
> The basic search is by city, state, price range, number of bedrooms and number of bathrooms, more criteria can be added. This site also lets you find a member real estate professional in a particular area. This is a great help if you are moving to another state.

In order to defeat this type of person, take control of the situation. Refuse to look at a home that does not meet your qualifications. Insist that the houses the agent wants to show you meet certain criteria. You will have to be firm on this. Most real estate agents mean no harm. They sincerely believe they know what is best for their clients—especially first time buyers. However, the agent will not be there when you have to pay the mortgage bill or realize that your new home is not really what *you* wanted.

I have found that setting the tone of the real estate agent-client relationship at the beginning helps. Tell the agent what you must have and the price range you are looking for. You may even put it in writing for the agent. Tell the agent that you are a busy person and will not waste your time or the agent's time by looking at homes that do not match your criteria. Finally, before going to any showing, review the details on the home. Real estate agents have access to detailed info on each home.

Changing Agents

When I first started looking for homes, I was too afraid that I would hurt the real estate agent's feelings if I said that she or he was just not working out and I needed someone else. (It was sort of like dumping a steady boyfriend for no reason.)

After having several near misses in buying the wrong house, I realized that the agent's feelings were not my concern. My priority had to be me and my family. Buying the wrong house can cause financial disaster. It can begin an avalanche of problems for a family, especially if you over-extend yourself financially or buy a house that needs expensive work. It is up to you to insist that the real estate agent respect your wishes, listen to your needs, and understand your financial limitations.

I have found that an honest approach of "I do not think I can work with you" is enough. In most cases, the agent that I rejected would not listen to me about what I could afford and continued to show me homes that were way over my budget.

The only problem with changing agents is that in some states, the agent who showed the house to the buyer first, gets some *or* all of the commission. This depends on local regulations, state laws, and the contract that the seller and the real estate agent signed.

Example:

Sam's brother-in-law Tom is a new real estate agent. Sam has been looking for a home with the help of Ms. Green, a local real estate agent. Sam doesn't really like Ms. Green. On Friday, Ms. Green showed him his dream home. On Saturday, Sam told Ms. Green he was no longer interested in working with her. On Monday, Sam made an offer on the dream home using his brother-in-law Tom, so that Tom would get the commission.

In some instances, Tom would not get the commission because Ms. Green showed the buyer the house first. This depends on local regulations, state laws, and the contract that the seller and the real estate agent signed.

WHO DOES THE REAL ESTATE AGENT WORK FOR

The biggest misconception with real estate agents is whom they actually work for. In some states, a real estate agent works for the interest of the seller, not the buyer. Again, this depends on local regulations, state laws, and the contract that the seller and the real estate agent signed. This is hard to believe when *your* real estate agent is so friendly, and so accommodating to what you want. He or she looks for properties to show you, chauffeurs you to those places, and is ready to assist you in making a selection and getting a mortgage. Your state's Real Estate Commission or licensing board requires that the buyers be treated fairly, but in reality, the motivation is how a real estate agent is paid.

In some states where the real estate agent legally works for the interest of the seller, a homebuyer can hire his or her own real estate agent (often called a *buyer's agent*) to represent him or her in finding a home and negotiating its purchase. In order to get this kind of representation, the buyer must pay a percentage or fee to the broker, in much the same way that the seller contracts for a specific commission percentage with an agent.

HOW REAL ESTATE AGENTS GET PAID

When a person wants to sell their home they usually contact a local real estate agent. The agent views the property, estimates what the selling price should be, and advises the seller of any other things that need to be done to the property to make it more saleable. The seller and the agent then sign a contract that the house will be *listed* by the agent and that the agent will receive a certain percentage of the selling price when the house *closes* (or sells). Generally, the contract will specify the length of time the agent has to sell the house, restrictions as to how it is listed, and any other issues relating to the particular situation.

When the property is sold, the seller's agent or listing agent who contracted with the seller, gets his or her percentage of commission. The seller's agent or listing agent then takes part of that amount and gives it to the buyer's agent. This percentage of the split is determined by prior agreement.

For the real estate agency, it is more profitable for one of its own real estate agents (who represent the buyer) to sell a property that was listed by another one of its real estate agents (who represent the seller). This way, the agency would get the entire percentage of the selling price as listed in the contract, as opposed to having to split it with an agent who works at another agency.

MULTIPLE LISTING SERVICES (MLS)

The *Multiple Listing Services* are standard throughout the country. They provide information to all real estate agents that are members of the local MLS, about every house that other MLS agents are selling. This gives the buyer the opportunity to see more houses. Agents who are MLS members agree to split a percentage of the commission from the sellers.

Most real estate agents in this country belong to a multiple listing group, which allows all properties for sale in a certain area to be sold by any other licensed agent. In the Chicago area, this produces large phone book size listings of homes on the market by price and location.

On the opposite end of MLS is what are usually called *Exclusive listings*. In an exclusive listing, one real estate agent is selling the property. Only he or she is allowed to show the property and the information is not provided to any other agents. With exclusive listings, the real estate agent gets the full commission when the house is sold.

COMPARABLES

The *comparable* is a dollar number that real estate agents use in determining what a particular house is worth. Bankers and home insurance companies also look at this number. The comparable amount is obtained by looking at the selling price of similar houses (judged by square footage, number of rooms, type of construction) in the same area, for a certain time period. The area can be a few blocks within a particular city or the closest properties in the rural areas. This gives the average value of that particular type of home or approximately how much it is worth.

When judging comparables, it is important to use the selling price. If you use the asking price, those sellers who list their homes at an over-inflated amount will skew the result. If you are reading the real estate ads for a particular area over a few months, you will get a feel for what houses are being priced. Some newspapers list the actual sale price a few months after the sale has been completed.

VIEWING A HOUSE UP FOR SALE

Driving in the area you want to live, you see a house with a 'for sale' sign. What do you do? Write down the address, name, and number on the sign. Sometimes there is a box affixed to the sign with an information sheet on the property (if you are just checking out the neighborhood, these sheets can be useful too). If you have an agent working for you, call him or her to obtain the information

ATTORNEY TIP:

Decide what are the top three items you MUST have in a house. When the real estate agent calls you to look at a particular house, ask if the house meets the three criteria. For example:

1) How much is the asking price?

2) Number of bedrooms?

3) Number of bathrooms?

If the answers do not conform to what you want, say "no thanks" to seeing that house.

on price, etc. Your agent may be able to schedule a time for you to see the home.

Notes and Checklists

Your real estate agent will have an *informational sheet* on each house he/she is planning to show you. Ask for your own copy. This sheet should have the *asking price*, number and sizes of rooms, size of the lot, sewage and water information, heating and cooling information, past taxes, and other positives of the house. Many of these listings include a picture of the property. Most times you will be seeing multiple homes each time you go out with your agent, so this information sheet will help you compare properties.

You should also keep a notebook for your notes on the property. This is something you can write on while actually looking at the home, or just after you have seen it. Keep notes on things that may be serious problems like the toilet does not flush; the water faucet does not shut off completely; one room is too cold or too hot; or, the furnace sounds strange. You may wish to use Worksheet 3 in Appendix D, page 173, in addition to your own notebook.

ATTORNEY TIP:

Insist that your real estate agent give you a copy of the informational sheet on each home you are seeing. This will give you a record of what you have looked at and a way to remind yourself about that particular house. This is also a test to see how cooperative the agent is with your needs.

Home Warranty

In some areas of the country, a warranty on a house being sold is an expected thing. It is a marketing tool meant to nudge the hesitant buyer to make an offer. However, the buyer cannot merely rely on this piece of paper for protection. You still must look at the home, negotiate for repairing defects, and above all, have that important home inspection.

Home warranties do not cover everything. If the buyer purchases a home that has a defect, which was disclosed by the seller, chances are the home warranty will not pay to have that defect fixed. Warranties, like contracts, are unique and it is impossible to make generalizations about what they cover. Usually a seller pays for the warranty, but may attempt to pass on the cost to the buyer as part of the deal.

ATTORNEY TIP:

Be a concerned consumer and don't rely on just one piece of paper. Read it. Ask questions. Then get that inspection.

WHAT NOT TO SAY TO REAL ESTATE AGENTS AND SELLERS

Never let your real estate agent know that you are willing to go higher in an offer for a home. The higher the selling price, the more commission they make. While it is not ethical, your real estate agent may be tempted to tell the sellers that you are willing to pay more.

As for the sellers, remember this is the seller's home. Do not criticize the decorating, the layout, the furniture, or anything else out loud. Make a note to discuss points later with your agent. In the same vein, do not discuss plans to knock down walls, rip out carpeting, tear down cabinets—out loud. Quietly observe each room and make notes. Do not make an enemy of the sellers. Be polite. If you can't say something nice don't say anything at all.

Most real estate agents will tell their sellers to leave the home while it is being shown. I personally find this practice very insensitive for the sellers

ATTORNEY TIP:

Remember that your real estate agent is being paid a percentage of the selling price. Real estate agents really want their clients to buy a home.

and extremely limiting for the buyers. To expect two families to negotiate the cost of a home without ever seeing each other is silly. Having been both seller and buyer, I have found that the deals went smoother when both sides at least saw each other once before the financial dealing.

GAMES PLAYED TO MAKE THE SALE

Be sure to review the earlier section on how real estate agents get paid. This will give you an idea of their motivation. It is more profitable if the same agency that lists the property also sells it. It is more profitable to sell the property at the highest amount possible. The majority of real estate agents do not defraud or purposely act in an irresponsible way in order to get the sale. However, the following are some of the more common *games* used to push a sale.

Inflating the Worth of the House

Real estate agents can inflate the worth of the house in a number of ways. One way is to show you houses listed at a higher price range than the homes are worth. These are the ones where the current owner, for whatever reason, has listed the asking price of the house at an over-inflated, amount. Once you have seen several over-priced houses, the agent shows you a house that is properly priced, but still in the same high price range.

There can be two problems here:

- the high-price range may be beyond what you want to pay and
- the over-priced homes you looked at may not be a good example of what is available for that price.

This manipulation makes the one properly-priced home look like a real steal.

Another way to inflate the worth of the house is to use the asking price of similar homes and not the selling price when making a comparable calculation. This makes homes look like they are worth more than the market value and again may push you into considering property above what you decided was your limit.

If you have questions about the worth of a particular house, ask that the real estate agent show you similar homes that have recently sold at a similar or comparable price. A real estate professional should be able and willing to give you this information. If yours is not, consider getting a different agent.

Another Offer

Real estate agents may also rush you to make an offer on a home by saying that they have heard that someone else is making an offer on that property right now, so you have to hurry. While there are times when a particular piece of property may be so desirable that people are standing in line to make an offer, that is the exception.

It has been my experience that each and every home I have ever considered making an offer on is just about to be snapped up by another person who is coincidentally ready to offer more. There always is another agent in the same office that is just about to seal the deal. While it may seem like gambling with losing a home you want, my response has always been "Good for them. I hope they get the house, but I need time to make a decision." This type of response lets your real estate agent know that they cannot bluff you and it allows you the time you need to decide on this home.

Another time a buyer is rushed is after the offer has been made. The sellers reject the offer and come back with a *counter offer* that is more money than you want to spend. I personally do not like playing games with a real estate purchase. When I make an offer on a property, it is usually fair and in accordance with what I believe the property is worth and what I can afford. If the seller counters with an amount that is outside of my budget or I feel is outrageous for the property, to me that is not acting in good faith and I look for another property.

Many real estate agents will urge you to meet the sellers offer, extend yourself more, and of course, do it right now. The buyer is urged to do this immediately before someone else buys the property—before you get a chance to think. Going up from a first offer, as long as that is appropriate for the house value and within your finances, is fine—as long as you are not pressured to make the decision.

This is one of the biggest decisions of your life and you do not need to be pushed into making it before you are ready. When you find the right home, you will not be asking for time to decide. The decision will feel right.

WHEN DO YOU LEGITIMATELY NEED TO ACT FAST

The fact is that there are some areas of the country where homes are sold within the first forty-eight hours of being put on the market. In that case, the real estate agent is 100% correct in urging the buyer to act fast.

One of the first homes that I bought and rehabbed had an offer within four hours of the home being put on the market—for the full asking price. There was no outward indication that my house would sell fast. Most other houses in that area were not selling in twenty-four hours. My house was correctly priced considering the area and the upgrades put into the house. However, the buyer lived close; and, had watched the upgrades and improvements made to my house. He was very motivated.

How do you know when to act fast to get a home? If you have been reading the real estate section of the paper for a particular area, you will have some indication as to how fast the homes move. Also, your real estate agent may be able to provide actual listings of homes that sold and how long they were on the market. Of course, remember that a neighbor down the block may have his eye on the place and will be making an offer on the house before you even get a chance to see it.

ATTORNEY TIP:

What is a buyer's market? What is a seller's market? Indicators of a buyer's market are homes that linger on the market for a long time before being sold; homes where the asking price has been reduced; and/or homes where the selling price is much lower than the asking price. In a seller's market, homes sell quickly—usually for the asking price or above.

If you want to buy in an area where homes are selling quickly, be prepared to pay the full asking price. Which, of course, means that when you are looking for a home, you use that asking price as a guide. Do not expect that you will be able to pay less.

chapter seven

Handling the Emotional Side of a Home Purchase

House hunting and buying is one of those times in your life when you need to be practical, logical, and unemotional. However, as luck would have it, this is the time when emotions often run high. Emotions can sabotage a first-time home buyer and cause mistakes.

Following are the common occasions when emotions can cause problems in buying your first home. Read this section carefully to learn what to expect, how to overcome potential problems, and when to take a time out.

EMOTIONS IN HOUSE HUNTING

Congratulations! You have decided which neighborhood you want to live in. It has everything you want—the schools are good, the people seem friendly, and the resale value of property is going up. The next hurdle—find your home.

Under a Deadline

If you are under pressure due to an expiring lease or problems where you are currently living, you may be eager to make an offer on the first house that is available. Before you make that jump, step back and review your worksheets of what you want to determine whether the house is right for you or if you are just rushing to get out of where you live. You may want to consider putting your belongings in storage and taking a temporary rental in a month-to-month residence to give you additional time to look for a home.

In my own experience, I had moved into a new city, rented an apartment, and began the search for a home. The rental was a disaster. It had a criminal element and roaches. I was in such a hurry to find a place to live that I made an offer on a home that I could move into it right away because the owners had already moved. Within the first month of my living there, I found out why the previous owners were so anxious to leave. The next door neighbors threw huge parties complete with live bands every weekend.

ATTORNEY TIP:

Buy yourself a good tape measure at the hardware store. Measure each room of where you currently live and write the room sizes down on an index card. When you are viewing a house up for sale, refer to this card to determine if you and your furniture will fit into the rooms.

The House is Beautifully Decorated

There is nothing more emotionally satisfying than seeing a home where everything is just perfect. The decorating in each room is exactly what you want. The furniture is exquisite. The kitchen smells of fresh cooked bread, and it looks like a spread in *House Beautiful.*

It shouldn't surprise you to know that real estate agents will work with the seller to present just this picture. What you need to do is look past the decorating, the soft music, and smell of warm bread. What will this house look like with your furniture, your clutter, your children, and the smell of your cooking?

One way to get away from being influenced by the seller's decoration is to concentrate on the size of each room and the square footage of the home. Before you even look at a home, measure the size of your current bedroom, bathroom, kitchen, and living area. These measurements will give you a starting point to judge other homes. If your current bedroom is so cramped with furniture that you only have a path around the bed, you have a guide as to how big the bedroom in the new house should be. I have found that measuring a room that I am familiar with is a much better gauge than a mere number of feet and inches.

It is a Real Steal

We all love sales and sometimes we buy things just because it is such a good price on sale. However, this is not the best advice to use when buying a home. You have selected the neighborhood, chosen the type of house, and then something sort of close to what you want is available at a price that is much less than other homes in this area. This is a very tough one for most of us to ignore.

The first question you need to get an answer for is "Why is this one home selling at such a low cost?" Your real estate agent may be able to get the answer, but don't count on it. Sometimes the sellers themselves will volunteer that they are relocating out of state, are getting a divorce, or have decided to retire. Sometimes the answer lies in the construction problems. If you cannot get an answer to your question and do plan to make an offer on the house, you need to make your offer contingent on the house passing an inspection.

If the inspection shows some defects, it is up to you to decide how important that defect is. Will the current owner fix this before the sale? Are you willing to pay to get the problem fixed or can you fix it yourself? Is the lender willing to loan you the amount you need to pay for the home? Does this home meet your criteria or are you willing to compromise for the low price?

In my case, after two months of looking, the real estate agent showed us a home that had been on the market for over a year—much longer than anything else. The owners were in a panic and had just significantly reduced the asking price. The home had suffered from a lot of neglect. One bedroom was painted all black. Cars were parked on the non-existent front lawn and every wall needed to be scrubbed with strong detergent. We looked at it from a non-emotional perspective. The neighborhood was right; the home had the number of rooms we wanted; the defects could be fixed; and, it was a good value for the money.

Using the Seller's Emotions

Remember that the seller is proud of their home. If you do encounter the sellers, keep any negative comments to yourself and find something to praise. Sellers want to hear complements—not how you are going to tear out all their decorating. This is one of those times when being nice really counts.

If you know why the sellers are moving, it may help you in dealing with them. Someone who is being forced to move because of finances or divorce is not likely to be very friendly. If you sense that this sale is not to move to a better life a simple "You have a beautiful home" will do. Sellers who are anxious to start a new life or are happily relocating can be a wealth of information on the house, what they did, what improvements they made, and the neighborhood.

You want the sellers to like you. Every real estate agent has a story of how the seller chose a particular buyer not because of the amount offered, but because of something intangible. Think about it, if two people come to buy your home for the same or close dollar amounts, who will you sell to—the person who is friendly or the one who is itching to strip the home of all of your hard work?

I have looked at homes where the sellers were arguing, where they refused to speak to my real estate agent, and where they followed me around as if I would take something. None of that kept me from looking at what was important to me and taking sufficient notes to make a decision. When the tour was over, I made sure I said something positive to the sellers; thanked

> **ATTORNEY TIP:**
>
> If you see the seller's neighbors watching you as you view the house, smile and nod at them. If you are really interested in the area, come back later (without your real estate agent) and speak to the neighbors.

them for letting me intrude; and, left. (Incidentally, the house where the seller followed me around was the one I selected.)

BUYERS REGRET / BUYERS REMORSE

You have undoubtedly heard the term *buyer's remorse*. It happens to everyone. No matter how unemotional and factual your decision to buy a house is, it will hit you. The feeling when you realize that you have just taken on an enormous debt for the rest of your life. For some people, this hits after you have signed the contract to offer the seller an amount. For some, it is after the sellers accept the offer. For many, it is at the closing. No matter who you are, buyer's regret will get you.

When this happens, refer back to the notes and information you have made on the property. Go over the reasons why you chose this particular house and try to concentrate on how you will make the place a home.

As to the total amount of money that will be paid over the mortgage, concentrate more on the monthly payments. It is required that a lender tell you how much the total money of principal and interest you will pay over the life of the mortgage. You will be glad to have the knowledge, however the total number is so big it could just as well be the national debt. Chances are that the majority of us who hear that number will

> **ATTORNEY TIP:**
>
> Three things to remember when looking at a house for sale when the sellers are there:
> - smile;
> - say something positive about the house; and,
> - whatever happens, keep your composure.

> **ATTORNEY TIP:**
>
> Quick cure for buyer's remorse.
>
> You know you are going to have this, so stock up on something to celebrate when you know that the seller has accepted your offer. A bottle of favorite wine, a box of expensive chocolates, a good steak — something to mark this as a celebration, not a time to be a "Monday morning quarterback."

sell that home and buy another one—pretty much living our entire lives in debt. As long as we want to move up to a better home this is the way it will be. While it would be great to pay off one mortgage before looking for a new home, don't expect that to happen.

Section Three:
Finances

chapter eight:
Explanation of Mortgage Basics

This chapter contains basic information and terms used in the mortgage industry. Finding the best mortgage for your situation also requires research.

Your real estate agent may be able to provide a list of lenders in the area who make mortgage loans or you may already have a business relationship with a bank, credit union, or financial institution. Be sure to get information on a mortgage from several lenders in order to make the right decision for you. Worksheet 4 in Appendix D, page 175 lists common points for comparing lenders. Make photocopies of this worksheet and start interviewing lenders.

PRE-QUALIFYING

Many mortgage lenders will allow a prospective borrower to *pre-qualify* for an estimated mortgage amount before they select a home. There are several advantages to doing this.

This may eliminate the house sale being held up for problems in obtaining a mortgage, which can make you very desirable from the seller's standpoint. In an area where many mortgages are being written, just the volume of these transactions can hold up house closings for days or even months. A buyer who is pre-qualified has already eliminated some of the potential for delays, which is a plus for the seller who needs to be out of the house by a certain date. In an area where homes sell fast, pre-qualification may be the thing that puts your offer ahead of others.

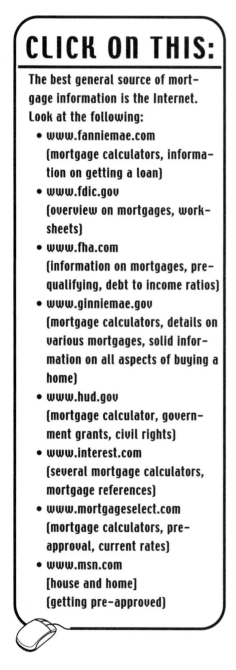

CLICK ON THIS:

The best general source of mortgage information is the Internet. Look at the following:

- www.fanniemae.com
  (mortgage calculators, information on getting a loan)
- www.fdic.gov
  (overview on mortgages, worksheets)
- www.fha.com
  (information on mortgages, pre-qualifying, debt to income ratios)
- www.ginniemae.gov
  (mortgage calculators, details on various mortgages, solid information on all aspects of buying a home)
- www.hud.gov
  (mortgage calculator, government grants, civil rights)
- www.interest.com
  (several mortgage calculators, mortgage references)
- www.mortgageselect.com
  (mortgage calculators, pre-approval, current rates)
- www.msn.com
  [house and home]
  (getting pre-approved)

Remember that you are pre-qualifying for an estimated amount. If you have had financial problems between the time you pre-qualify and the actual mortgage application, the lender may lower the amount they are willing to lend.

Additionally, a mortgage is also based on the property that you want to purchase. If the lender believes that the property is not worth the mortgage amount or if there are serious defects in the home or serious problems in the neighborhood, the lender may not be willing to base a mortgage on that purchase. A pre-qualification amount may be stated as a range amount. Remember, a pre-qualification is NOT a guarantee or a loan commitment.

PRE-APPROVAL

Pre-approval is a more formal process. The lender examines your finances in detail and legally agrees to loan you a certain amount of money. Not all lenders do formal pre-approvals, because when you obtain a mortgage the value of the property is a very large factor in the total amount of a loan you can get. In some areas of the country, pre-approvals are totally non-existent.

Pre-approvals are more extensive and more detailed than pre-qualification. More information is required from the potential borrower. The time it takes to process a pre-approval is longer than for pre-qualification. However, borrowers with pre-approvals can cut the time waiting for a mortgage approval, considerably.

MORTGAGE LENDER TYPES

For most of us who want a mortgage, the *type* or *classification* of lender is not an issue. Lower interest rates and the increase in mortgage activity has blurred the lines between the traditional classifications. However you may want to review the types of lenders to see how they fit your needs.

Portfolio Lenders

These are usually banks and savings & loan institutions. The term portfolio comes because the loans are made from the lender's own portfolio of assets and usually not for resale in the secondary market. You may not know the type of mortgage lender that you are dealing with because these classifications have become blurred. If your real estate agent recommends a particular lender, it will probably be worthwhile to use that lender. Many real estate professionals have developed relationships with mortgage lenders that help in getting their clients approved with the least amount of red tape—in the least amount of time.

However, even true portfolio lenders may sell a mortgage on the secondary market after a year or more of mortgage payments. Portfolio loans are typically easier to qualify for and as such do not always offer those great competitive rates. As many portfolio lenders have begun to engage in mortgage banking, those things that made this type of lender different have begun to disappear.

Mortgage Bankers

The larger institutions that do much of the volume mortgage work are called *mortgage bankers*. Some mortgage bankers may offer first-time buyer programs through the state and local government programs. While these large institutions have a lot of clout in working with FHA and VA programs, remember you are dealing with a large bureaucratic company.

Direct Lender

Like portfolio lenders, *direct lenders* fund their own mortgage loans from their own portfolio. In the past direct lenders always used their own name on the loan documents. Now, even the smallest mortgage broker can arrange to fund a loan in their own name. A direct lender can be one of the biggest lenders to the smallest. Some direct lenders are actually mortgage bankers.

Mortgage Brokers

Loan officers who represent several companies that offer mortgage loans are called *mortage brokers*. The broker has the flexibility to match a buyer with the right lender. If the buyer is denied a mortgage the broker can merely submit the loan documents to another lender.

CLICK ON THIS:

The Internet sites www.fha.com and www.interest.com provide a lot of information on the various types of mortgages and will help you select the one right for you.

MORTGAGE TYPES

Following are some of the most common mortgage types. These are not all the mortgage types available, as many lending institutions create their own mortgages.

Adjustable Rate Mortgage (ARM)

An *Adjustable Rate Mortgage (ARM)* has varying interest rates depending on a particular

Index. The Index is a measurement of the economy that is published by reliable financial groups. Common indexes are U.S. Treasury Bills and the Federal Housing Finance Board's Contract Mortgage Rate. The index is not under the control of the lender, but is driven by the economy in general.

Because the interest rate of an *ARM (Adjusted Rate Mortgage)* is tied to an index, the interest rate, and therefore the monthly payments, are variable. ARMs usually have *caps*, which is the highest that the interest can go up to. However, some caps are only set for the amount the interest can rise annually. This means if the cap is 2% annually with no other restriction, the interest could go up that much every year. Most ARMs recalculate on an annual or semi-annual basis after the first couple of years of payment.

The ARM usually starts out at a very low interest rate, which makes it attractive. However, these low rates are only temporary. A borrower with a small down payment or less than stellar credit rating may be able to qualify for an ARM easier than a fixed rate mortgage because of the low initial payments. ARMs are based on the theory that everyone's salary will increase over successive years.

Assumable Mortgages

When interest rates for mortgages are going up, a mortgage with a lower interest rate becomes very desirable. One way to get a mortgage at this lower rate is to take-over the existing mortgage on a home. This is called *assuming the mortgage* of another.

Traditionally, both *Federal Housing Administration (FHA)* and *Veterans Administration (VA)* loans are assumable. Other lending institutions may also offer assumable loans. In recent years, mortgage interest rates have continued to decrease. If the country ever goes into another period of inflation that causes the interest rates to increase, we will be looking for assumable mortgages with the 2003 rates.

Balloon Mortgages

Balloon mortgages are like ARMs because the interest offered may be low. However, the loan is only financed for a short period of time, with the most common being seven years. At the end of the seven years, the borrower must pay a very large *balloon payment*. Because this lump-sum balloon payment is so large, most borrowers will then be forced to find another mortgage.

Balloon mortgages can be written with various terms, some of which only benefit the lender. Before you consider this type of mortgage, know what the terms are and how they will effect your payments.

Buydown Mortgage

Some lending institutions offer a method to reduce the interest rate and the monthly mortgage payments. This type of *buydown mortgage* can require a sum of money up front in addition to a down payment or at the end of the mortgage as in a balloon payment. The calculations differ from place to place. This form of mortgage is usually not used when mortgage interest rates are low.

Convertible ARM

A *Convertible ARM* is an Adjustable Rate Mortgage that can be changed into a fixed rate mortgage upon a certain event. Usually, the ability to convert the mortgage is tied to mortgage interest rates, a government index amount, or a period of time.

Deferred Interest Mortgage

A *Deferred Interest Mortgage* allows payments made in the beginning of the mortgage to go primarily toward paying down the principal. This is a variation of the balloon mortgage, because at some point the deferred interest amount will need to be paid.

Fixed-Rate Mortgage

A *Fixed Rate-Mortgage* is the most popular type of mortgage. The interest stays the same throughout the entire term of the mortgage—usually fifteen or thirty years. The monthly mortgage payments are the same amount over the term of the mortgage. This fixed amount allows the borrower to budget easier and protects the borrower against inflation.

15-Year Mortgage vs. 30-Year Mortgage

A 15-year mortgage has a lower, overall cost due to the lower interest rate. The short term of the loan means that the home-owner will build equity in the home quicker and the debt will only last for fifteen years. On the negative side, 15-year mortgage means higher monthly payments. The lower interest rate means a lesser amount can be deducted from your annual income tax.

A 30-year mortgage has lower monthly payments. This type of mortgage is easier to qualify for and allows the homeowner to take more tax deductions over the length of the mortgage. Of course, the big difference is the length of time you will be paying mortgage payments. Because this type of mortgage has a higher interest rate, the homebuyer will actually pay more for the home than if the buyer got a 15-year mortgage.

Wraparound Mortgage

The *Wraparound Mortgage* is the result of an agreement between the seller and the buyer. The buyer pays a certain number of mortgage payments for the seller, plus the buyer obtains his own mortgage. This may also be called *seller financing*.

Buyers who do not qualify for a mortgage on the full selling price of the home benefit from this. The buyer pays the old mortgage for a period of time and then applies for his/her own mortgage on the lower selling price.

If you are considering doing this type of transaction, get the help of a real estate attorney to draft a contract between you and the seller.

ATTORNEY TIP:

There are many potential pitfalls with a Wraparound Mortgage. Do not attempt to work with this type of mortgage without the assistance of an experienced attorney.

NECESSARY DOCUMENTS TO APPLY FOR A MORTGAGE

Once you decide on a lender, you will be asked to fill out a mortgage application and provide financial information to the lender. Most lenders ask for certain financial records when you apply for a mortgage. These records fall into two categories: income and expenses. Following is a list of what most lenders require; however, your particular lender may require more information.

Income:
- pay check stubs;
- W-2s for the past two years;
- income tax returns;
- proof of alimony/child support (divorce decree);
- dividends;
- investments;
- bank statements;
- an estimated value of your other assets;
- location of checking and savings accounts; and,
- copy of document indicating how much earnest money you put down.

Expenses:
Lenders will request their own credit report on you, but may also require that you list all your outstanding debts.

Other:
- the address where you lived for the last two years;
- your employer and salary over the last five years;
- number of people who will live in the home; and,
- names of closest relative not living with you.

Remember to check with your lender to see exactly what paperwork is required. While the above list is long, it likely does not cover every situation.

INTERNET MORTGAGES

We have all seen the obnoxious man who pitches Internet mortgages on TV commercials. The question is "Does this really work?" The answer is "sometimes."

While doing your research on the Internet, you will run across many ads for mortgages. You probably should be more cautious with an Internet mortgage company than you would be in buying software from an Internet company. Do research and ask questions. You may also want to contact the Better Business Bureau or State Consumer Fraud Department. Because this a new area of business, there is not a lot known about the stability of the Internet mortgage companies.

CLICK ON THIS:

One way to protect yourself from mortgage fraud (Internet or otherwise), is to learn the warning signs of fraud in lending. The best website for this information is www.stopmortgagefraud.com.

YOUR MORTGAGE IS NOT APPROVED

What happens if you have done all the hard work in choosing a lender, gone through the torture of filling out the mortgage application, and you are not approved?

First, try to find out why you were denied. Was the property appraised lower than the amount you wanted to borrow? In that case, maybe you should re-think your house selection. If you still want that property, you will need to

ATTORNEY TIP:

You just got a call from the lending institution that you were not approved for your mortgage. How do you respond?

The most important thing:

Ask why you were turned down. If the person on the phone cannot tell you why, ask to speak to someone who can tell you, even if that means the bank president.

In order to determine what your next step is, you need to know why you were turned down.

increase your down payment in order to reduce the amount borrowed.

This is a serious warning. The lender has contracted with a professional to appraise the property. If that professional sees problems with the house, perhaps those problems are something that have been missed. Be wary of proceeding with such a purchase. Make sure that you know why the appraiser valued the property that way, for example, is it the structure or the neighborhood?

Other common reasons for being turned down for a mortgage are:

- a poor credit report, and/or,
- insufficient income for the amount of debt.

Again, try to get as much information on this denial as possible. Perhaps there was an error on the credit report or you neglected to include all the income you receive. If there are no obvious errors, perhaps the lending institution is seeing a problem in your ability to make that level of payments. You may need to rethink the price of homes you are looking at. You can always go to another lender or increase the down payment so that the loan amount is lower.

A *mortgage broker* can present you to many suitable lenders. The broker knows which lenders accept "slightly tarnished" borrowers. If you decide to work with a broker, choose a reputable one. Ask for references, and **do not** pay any fees to the broker to handle your loan application.

Sometimes the lending institution denies someone a mortgage due to discrimination for such things as race, sex, ethnicity, religion, etc. If you feel you may have been discriminated against, you may be able to get assistance from the local HUD office.

CLICK ON THIS:

The HUD Internet site provides a wealth of information on how to battle discrimination in housing. View this at www.hud.gov or www.ginniemae.gov.

POINTS

In obtaining a mortgage you will hear the term *points* or *discount points*. This is an odd term for a totally illogical concept. The point in a mortgage is equivalent to 1% of the loan amount. The borrower usually pays this amount when he or she takes out the mortgage. For example, for a mortgage on a $100,000 home, each point would cost $1,000. The points would reduce the loan's interest rate by 0.125%.

The mortgage lenders use points as a type of up front discount and tie them to the interest rate of the mortgage. Using our $100,000 home example, the lender might offer a mortgage with a rate of 8.0% and no points, or 7.875% with one point, or 7.75% with two points. Points can make a mortgage rate appear low, while in reality the actual amount paid to the lender is higher because of a large number of points that must be paid.

Points are usually an up front payment made at the time you purchase the house. This is *in addition* to the amount of down payment and other closing costs. However, because of borrower's demand, many lenders will allow the borrower to finance all or part of the point's amount over the term of the mortgage.

Should you pay points up front or finance them? The answer is up to the individual. Paying more toward the mortgage up front will lower monthly payments. However, paying more at closing leaves the homebuyer with less cash at a time when the costs of moving into a new home can be overwhelming.

chapter nine:

Government Agencies and the Secondary Mortgage Market

HUD, *FHA*, *Fannie Mae*, *Ginnie Mae*, and *Freddie Mac* are names batted around by lenders and real estate professionals as though everyone knows what they are. They all have to do with financing and the very, very lucrative business of providing mortgages.

HOUSING & URBAN DEVELOPMENT AGENCY (HUD)

HUD's primary purpose is to provide mortgage insurance through the *Federal Housing Administration (FHA)*. The FHA will pay the mortgage if the borrower cannot. HUD offers special home buying programs for which you may qualify. Many of these are offered in conjunction with your local government. These programs provide some financial assistance and financial counseling for those who find themselves in trouble because of debt.

CLICK ON THIS:

As the name suggests, HUD is a department of the US government. HUD has numerous plans. HUD's website is a wealth of information to anyone who is considering buying a home. Spend some time reviewing this information at www.hud.gov. It is well worth it.

HUD provides education and information for everyone who wants to buy a home. HUD may even be able to pick up some of your closing costs if you buy a HUD home.

A HUD home is a *foreclosure* from someone who had a HUD mortgage and was not able to keep up with the payments. The homes range in price, but can suffer from neglect or be in less desirable neighborhoods. HUD homes are sold on an *as is* basis, which means that HUD will not correct defects even if they are obvious. This is why HUD homes are sold at such a low price. HUD does not have to spend money to fix them.

ATTORNEY TIP:

If you are considering buying a HUD home, you will need a real estate agent to process a bid on the home. You may also want to hire an attorney who specializes in this type of transaction.

Before you buy a HUD home, make sure you know what you are doing, especially in repairs. HUD lists these foreclosures at their offices, on their web site, and in local papers.

HUD also helps those have been discriminated in housing to get justice. Additionally, HUD assists the homeless and low-income people by providing vouchers for those with below poverty income and by supporting many non-profit organizations.

FEDERAL HOUSING ADMINISTRATION (FHA)

The FHA is actually an agency of HUD. FHA insures mortgage loans for HUD. If you apply for a mortgage that is insured by the FHA, it is called an FHA loan. Both the property and you will be required to qualify.

FHA loans allow a smaller down payment and come in a variety of loan types from the standard fixed-rate to those with interest rates that vary depending

CLICK ON THIS:

Visit www.hud.gov or www.fha.com for more specific information on FHA loans.

upon a financial index. Besides low down payments, an FHA loan places limits on fees and closing costs—all of which are financial benefits for the first-time home buyer.

GINNIE MAE

The *Government National Mortgage Association* or *Ginnie Mae* is a government owned corporation under HUD. Its purpose is to provide assistance to low and moderate income homebuyers. As with Fannie Mae, Ginnie Mae is able to generate profits by investing in the secondary mortgage market. The difference is that Ginnie Mae only deals with government-backed securities. This organization also provides money for low cost, affordable housing and community development.

CLICK ON THIS:

For more information about government-backed securities loans, visit the following site: www.ginniemae.gov.

FANNIE MAE

The *Federal National Mortgage Association (FNMA)* or *Fannie Mae* was created by Congress to bolster the housing industry in the 1920s. Now it is a private corporation that receives no government funding.

It is the largest source of home mortgage funds. It receives its profits from investments in the secondary mortgage market. It is also a leader in providing funds for affordable housing and investments in community development, especially in economically disadvantaged areas.

CLICK ON THIS:

For more information about Fannie Mae loans, visit www.fanniemae.com.

More information for the first-time home buyer can be found at www.freddiemac.com.

FREDDIE MAC

The *Federal National Mortgage Association (FNMA)* or *Freddie Mac* is a congressionally created corporation, that is in the business of buying and selling mortgages. This ultimately puts more funds for mortgages in the market place. Like its sisters Fannie Mae and Ginnie Mae, Freddie Mac provides mortgage money in areas that are economically disadvantaged and has been successful in lowering interest rates.

SECONDARY MORTGAGE MARKET

If you are wondering how these companies can afford to stay in business, it is because of investments in the *secondary mortgage market*. To explain this in the easiest of terms think back to the mortgage contract that a borrower signs with the lender. This contract says that the borrower will pay back the amount loaned, plus a percentage of interest. If the borrower cannot pay back the loan, then the lender takes back the home.

Generally, the loan is not for the full market value of the house. Also, real estate values usually increase over time. Therefore, if the lender does have to take the house back (foreclosure) he or she can resell it for the amount owed on the loan, plus profit.

In addition, the two major parts of a mortgage—the *principal* amount and the *interest*—are paid in *disproportionate* amounts. In the beginning, the mortgage payment is almost all interest with a small amount going against principal. As time goes on, the amount of money that goes against the principal increases, as the amount going against the interest decreases. The majority of the lender's profit comes from the interest. In the way mortgage payments are structured, the lender gets his or her profit first, so in case of a foreclosure the lender has already received a good portion of the expected profit.

The mortgage contract is valuable because the holder of this contract gets expected profits, even if there is a foreclosure. The mortgage becomes a thing of value because of what it represents and because it can be bought and sold. Some lenders package or group a certain number of mortgages together and sell them through companies like Freddie Mac. By packaging mortgages in groups the lender can put mortgages made to those with shaky credit history in a group with mortgages for people that are expected to make every payment. That way the mortgage lender gets all of its profit, less discounts, up front. The sale gives the lender more cash to make more mortgages.

Companies like Freddie Mac repackage the mortgages that they bought from multiple lenders and sell this new package to another mortgage lender. This can go on for as many mortgage lenders and companies who invest in the secondary market. Freddie Mac also sells *notes* (financial loans) which are backed by multiple mortgage loans to people who invest in securities. Freddie Mac takes its profits and invests them in purchasing more loans, which puts more available mortgage money into the economy.

The fact is that as each company or lender makes a sale, it gets funds to invest in more mortgages. This keeps the flow of money for mortgages available, even when the economy has problems.

ATTORNEY TIP:

The Internet sites mentioned in this chapter attempt to explain the complex world of the secondary mortgage market. While it is not essential that you understand this method of high finance in order to buy a home, you should understand the meaning of the terms that real estate professionals use in their discussions with you.

For the borrower, having your mortgage sold usually only means that you send your payments to a different address. Of course, each lender will provide different services. One may provide envelopes and coupons for each payment; another may send a monthly bill. If a borrower learns that his/her mortgage has been sold, it is the borrower's responsibility to learn what the new lender requires.

chapter ten:
Additional Sources of Money

The fact is that the higher the down payment you make, the lower the monthly mortgage payment will be. Since a mortgage payment is not just the amount to repay the loan, (but also usually includes home insurance and taxes which both increase over the years), the less you have to pay on the loan the better. Besides funds for down payments, you may be able to get help with low interest loans or community funds.

FRIENDS & RELATIVES

One place to get money to increase your down payment is from your relatives. Parents may be willing to give you an amount against a future inheritance, a substantial gift, or even a loan. Along with parents, perhaps a relative may be willing to loan you some money, especially if you sign a *promissory note* that includes a payback with interest.

Many young couples who are about to be married make a deal with their parents to forego the expensive wedding reception in lieu of that amount of money toward a down payment. I have been at weddings where the bride and groom requested cash toward their home instead of gifts or where the newlyweds put the money they would have spent on a lavish honeymoon into their down payment.

Example:

Ginny and Leo wanted to get a house within one year after they married. Ginny had saved enough money for a very expensive designer wedding dress and her parents offered to pay for the wedding reception. Leo's parents had very little extra money, but offered to pay for the honeymoon. Ginny and Leo decided that they wanted a home more than a big wedding reception. They went to their relatives and asked for help.

The family offered to all pitch in to give the young couple an old fashioned wedding reception. Uncle Bob donated the Moose hall. Aunt Deedee, Aunt Edith, and Aunt Marian cooked the food. Uncle George got a friend to donate the wedding cake and Uncle Marty provided cases of beer and wine.

Ginny wore her grandmother's wedding dress. They honeymooned in a cottage owned by Leo's cousin, Sam. By including the entire family Ginny and Leo were able to save enough money for a sizeable down payment on their dream home.

RETIREMENT SAVINGS

If your employer has a 401k, stock incentive, or savings plan, you may be able to use part of that money for your down payment. However, beware of the taxes. Before you make plans to cash-in this retirement nest egg, know what taxes and penalties you will be responsible for. Besides the potential for a sizeable penalty or tax bill, your employer may also have restrictions on how much you can reduce this fund and when you can do it. It may become a loan that will be deducted from your paycheck.

A word about cashing in your retirement funds. A good (sizable) down payment is definitely the way to go, but if it means that you have no retirement savings and nothing except the house to fall back on, make sure you know all consequences. Retirement funds are great sources for major emergencies, death, severe illness, and for that time when you no longer want to or can work. Weigh this before you deplete your entire retirement survival fund.

Many senior citizens are forced to sell their beloved homes because social security payments do not cover normal expenses plus property tax increases. Keep some savings for the senior time of your life.

Some companies provide credit unions for employees. A credit union may be able to handle your mortgage or provide you with a low interest loan for your down payment.

LOCAL GOVERNMENT ASSISTANCE

Some states, counties, and cities offer financial assistance for homebuyers under special circumstances. Usually this money is specifically for those areas where the structures are run down and the city wants to rebuild the neighborhood. These are typically the homes that have been abused and neglected. Low cost loans are offered if the buyer commits to rehabbing the structure and then using it as their primary residence. Along with city money for rehabbing, structures that hold certain significance (usually historical) or are in a historical landmark area may qualify for assistance from preservation groups.

Example:

The City of Chicago recently held a seminar for the first-time homebuyer. The seminar was directed toward the buyer who would rehab or fix up a city property. Besides an overview of how much work it takes to rehab a house, the city brought in both lending institutions that were willing to write low cost mortgages and federal agencies that also could provide funding.

The state of Illinois, through the Illinois State Treasurer, has a statewide program called "Our Own Home." This provides assistance for first-time homebuyers. The homebuyers must meet certain criteria to qualify for this program, but those that qualify will receive financial help from the state. This help is not in the form of money, but in the form of the state backing the homebuyer that may not qualify for regular mortgages. Even if you do not live in Illinois the Internet site **www.ourownhome.net**

contains Mortgage Calculators, Mortgage Glossary, and a list of Consumer Counseling Centers.

California assists home buyers in certain communities with various financial incentives. Buyers employed as teachers are among those eligible. For example, teachers may be eligible to receive a 50% discount on qualified homes for a down payment of $100.

The federal government also has assistance programs. For example, The *Department of Housing and Urban Development* (HUD) has a program called *Community Building* that may provide down payment assistance. Your state housing authorities may also have programs that will offer some assistance.

Again, the Internet is your best source for information on national or federal programs. Your state may have departments for housing authority or resident benefits that can assist you in finding state run programs. Local city government offices should have information on local programs. Real estate professionals should be able to assist you in this within the area that they serve.

ZERO DOWNPAYMENT

Yes, you read that right. Putting nothing down or a 100% mortgage. There are some lenders who are offering to finance 100% of the cost of a home. As with any too-good-to-be-true offer, there are some restrictions.

First, both the buyer and the property need to qualify. For the buyer, this may mean a totally spotless credit record and a really good, secure job. The property will need to be accurately appraised at an amount that is higher than the selling price. (This does happen frequently, especially in an area where house prices are showing steady increases.)

Second, the buyer will be required to purchase *Private Mortgage Insurance* or *PMI*. Note that many lenders require PMI purchase for anyone who puts down less than 20%. PMI charges an additional amount per month to insure that the mortgage will be paid.

Example:

Currently, in the Chicago area, the Private Mortgage Insurance monthly payment on a house which sells for $100,000 is approximately $65 per month with a 5% down payment. The same house is approximately $88 per month with a zero down payment on the mortgage.

Zero down payment loans are available in areas where the price of homes are increasing. Experts predict that this type of creative financing will continue to expand as long as housing values continue to be higher than mortgage values.

LOW INTEREST MORTGAGES

Another way to approach this is to get a mortgage which requires less of a down payment. Read Chapters 9 and 11 on government insured mortgages, *FHA,* and *VA loans.* Both of these require a lower down payment than *conventional mortgages.* There are also some private insurance companies that may allow you to finance your down payment. Real estate agents and brokers should be able to tell you if this is available in your area.

RENTING WITH AN OPTION TO BUY

One way a first-time homebuyer can build up a down payment is get into a *rent with option to buy* agreement. This type of arrangement may be non-existent where you live. You may want to seek the help of a real estate agent to find this type of situation.

In a *rent with an option to buy,* a percentage of your monthly rent is considered part of the down payment to purchase the home. The rental contract will last for a period of time and at the end of

CLICK ON THIS:

Great site to calculate down payment, closing costs, and how to get the money:

www.freddiemac.com

that time the renter then decides if he or she wants to buy. If the decision is not to buy, the renter does not get that percentage of the rent back.

Example:

Sally wanted to buy a new condominium close to her office, but she had saved only a small amount for a down payment. The condominium owner contracted with Sally to rent with an option to buy at the end of three years. The rent amount was a little higher than what Sally would be paying for similar condos. Sally's landlord would credit 25% of each monthly rent payment toward a down payment. At the end of three years, Sally had a credited $15,000 down payment from her rent.

chapter eleven:
VA Guaranteed Home Loans

One of the benefits of serving our country in the military is the *Veterans Administration Home Loan Guaranty Services.* This is part of the package of veteran's benefits and services that is administered by the Veterans Administration.

A VA guaranteed home loan is a regular mortgage or loan made by a lender. The lender can be a mortgage company, bank, or savings and loan. The big difference is that the Veterans Administration (VA) guarantees that the loan will be repaid if the borrower does not make the mortgage payments. This encourages lenders to offer VA loans by limiting their financial risk.

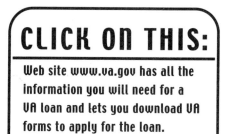

CLICK ON THIS:

Web site www.va.gov has all the information you will need for a VA loan and lets you download VA forms to apply for the loan.

QUALIFYING

To obtain a VA guaranteed loan, the veteran must first qualify. Length of service and the type of discharge determine this. Your local VA office will have the details of qualification. See Appendix E on page 179 for specific details of qualification for a VA guaranteed loan.

Generally, service qualifications require active duty of at least ninety days during wartime, 181 days during peacetime, or six years in the selected reserves or National Guard. Discharge from service must not be for dishonorable conditions. Widows and widowers of those killed in action and the spouses of POWs and MIAs may also qualify. (Children of veterans do not qualify for this entitlement.)

Because the details of qualification are very extensive, you should review them on the Internet (at **www.va.gov** in the home loan section) or by requesting VA Pamphlet 26-4 "VA-Guaranteed Home Loans for Veterans" and 26-6 "To the Home-Buying Veteran" from your local VA office. If you are currently on active duty or in the reserves, you can obtain all the information from your benefits coordinator.

If you qualify for a VA loan, the next step is to file VA form 26-1880 *Request of Certificate of Eligibility* (see copy in Appendix E on page 188). Many lenders can provide this form. The completed form plus copies of your discharge papers will be submitted to the Veteran's Administration for processing.

If you are currently in the military you are required to submit a Statement of Service. Statements of Service identify you by social security number, date of entry into the military, and the name of the base or command. It is signed by the appropriate officer, usually the CO, adjutant, personnel officer, or higher headquarters (depending on the branch of service.)

The VA will process your request and, if you are indeed eligible, will send you the Certificate.

VA APPRAISAL

Besides the borrower qualifying to be eligible for a VA guaranteed loan, the property must also qualify. The property qualifies on the basis of a VA appraisal. A VA appraisal estimates the value of the property. The appraisal results in a *Certificate of Reasonable Value* or *CRV*. The loan amount cannot exceed the CRV.

The request for a VA appraisal can come from anyone who is involved with the sale. Many lenders automatically do this for the military. You can request a VA appraisal by completing form VA 26-1805 *"Request for Determination of Reasonable Value."* The form is then sent to the nearest VA office/loan guarantee division. The VA assigns and pays for the appraisal. (A sample of this form with instructions begins in Appendix E on page 180.)

This appraisal is similar to that for HUD or FHA. The VA states that the primary reason for this appraisal is to make sure that the loan does not exceed the value of the house. It is not an inspection and does not guarantee that the property is free of problems. In fact, the VA encourages the borrower to get the house inspected prior to committing to an offer. In actual practice, this appraisal does help the borrower determine if the house is really worth the asking price.

> **ATTORNEY TIP:**
>
> The most important requirement for a VA loan is for the veteran to qualify. Those who have been discharged for reasons other than "Honorably" will not even be considered for this benefit.

My own experience with VA loans came when my parents were about to buy what looked like the most beautiful home ever built. Everything looked perfect and we all anticipated a move. That was until the VA appraiser refused to give the property a CRV.

The appraiser found extensive water damage hidden behind brand new wallpaper, plus blatant building code violations. The appraiser would not give the property a CRV unless the owner reduced the price or paid for repairs. We didn't get the house.

THE LOAN

The loan itself can be up to a maximum of $240,000 depending on the borrower's income, debts, and the appraised value of the house. VA guaranteed loans can be obtained for buying a house, townhouse, manufactured home, or condominium. This includes building a home and purchasing, plus rehabbing an existing home at the same time. A VA guaranteed loan can also be used to install certain energy efficient features or to refinance an existing home loan.

Veterans earn entitlements to VA guaranteed loans of a certain amount. This amount can be spread across two actual mortgages. In some instances, veterans who have prior outstanding VA loans may still be able to get a second loan. Because the entitlement amount has been increased over the years, you may want to check with the VA, even if you already have a VA loan.

ATTORNEY TIP:

If you are considering a VA loan, be sure to check for procedures and processes through your local VA office.

Generally, if your prior VA loan was foreclosed on, you will not be able to get another VA loan until that first amount is repaid to the VA. This can also be the case when a veteran's first VA loan was assumed and the person who assumed the loan defaulted.

Approval

Loan approval by the lender for a VA loan is almost identical to that for any other loan, just with a few extra steps.

- The applicant must be eligible and prove it by the Certificate of Eligibility.
- The loan must be for an eligible purpose (see above).
- The veteran must intend to live in the property as his or her primary residence.
- The veteran must be a satisfactory credit risk (the income must be stable and sufficient to meet the current debt plus the loan payments).
- The property must pass a VA appraisal and receive a CRV.

Advantages

A VA guaranteed loan is a good deal for the veteran. While obtaining a VA guaranteed loan on a particular property may take longer than conventional mortgage approval, it is worth the inconvenience for the advantages to the veteran.

Some of the positives of a VA guaranteed loan for the veteran:
- right to repay the loan at anytime without penalty;
- personal loan servicing and financial counseling to avoid foreclosure;
- a small or no down payment is required (as long as the value of the property and the income of the buyer is sufficient);
- low debt-to-income ratio;
- the loan maximum can be 100% of the property value;
- the interest rate can be negotiated;
- monthly mortgage insurance is not required;
- loan is assumable;
- traditional fixed rate with a choice of repayment plans; and,
- limited closing costs to the buyer.

Disadvantages

There are some real estate professionals who prefer not to use a VA loan because of the disadvantages to the seller. Remember this is not a hand out or charity, it is part of a big "thank you for your service" that is well earned by those in the military. If you qualify for and want to use the VA guaranteed loan entitlement, make your real estate agent aware of your intention at the beginning of your search. There are many real estate agents who are willing to cooperate in obtaining a VA loan.

That being said, a large percentage of sellers will list their property with a provision that they are not interested in selling to someone who is using FHA or VA guaranteed loans. In an economy or a neighborhood where homes sell fast, VA loans like FHA loans are not always welcome.

There are several reasons for this dislike of VA and FHA loans. One of the primary reasons is the extra time both of these loans take to close. In some areas of the country where homes do not stay on the market longer than a week, the private mortgage lenders have stepped up their service and can close the deal in about a month.

Besides the additional time it takes to close a VA or FHA loan, it also costs the seller more in closing costs because of the limitations on what closing costs the buyer pays. If the buyer wants the home and the seller does not want to accept a VA or FHA loan, a way to get around the additional closing costs is for the buyer to reimburse the seller for those out of ordinary closing costs in a separate deal.

Both VA and FHA require appraisals that may uncover something about the property which the sellers need to fix. The VA and FHA require that the house be appraised at an amount which is equal to the amount of the loan. While these appraisals result in determining the reasonable value of the home, the home must also adhere to certain construction standards set by VA and FHA.

One interesting thing has come out of the construction standards which the VA and FHA use. More conventional lenders are beginning to look at appraisals for these same items before they agree to write a mortgage on the home.

Even home insurance providers are requiring that certain items meet these tough standards before obtaining full insurance. My own home insurance company would not insure the garage on my property until the exterior walls were repaired, a door put on, and the structure reinforced. The same restrictions that both FHA and VA would have used.

SECTION FOUR:
THE BUYING PROCESS

chapter twelve:
The Legal Side
of Real Estate

Real estate transactions are getting more and more complex. More states counties and cities are enacting laws which effect what is required to sell the property and how much it will cost. Besides the complexity of the laws, the forms required just to make an offer and those used to apply for a mortgage have become so detailed that it would take hours just to read every word.

This chapter also provides an overview about the common ways to hold title. Each state has enacted laws that govern how title is held. Real estate attorneys are familiar with the requirements of both state and local laws and can advise you accordingly.

DO I NEED AN ATTORNEY

Before you sign an offer on a home, you may want an attorney to review it to make sure that your interests are protected. If you don't have an attorney before you sign the offer, you may ask to have a clause inserted in the offer contract that will allow an attorney to review the document and cancel the contract if there are items detrimental to your interests. Some areas of the country have a legal time period that is allowed for attorney review, the time period is usually a few days.

If you have obtained an attorney at the beginning of your home search, he or she can negotiate the agreement for sale, review the documents, and may be able to hold your escrow amount.

If you obtain an attorney after the offer contract has been accepted by the seller, the attorney can review the documents of the loan, perform title searches, order inspections, obtain land surveys, inform you as to how much money you must bring to closing, review all documents, and assist you in the closing so that you are signing the proper documents.

Many attorneys specialize in real estate closings. Most real estate agents have a list of referrals or you can obtain a referral from your local bar association.

TITLE SEARCHES AND SURVEYS

Depending on the area of the county, your attorney may be the one who orders a *title search* and *survey* of the property. A title search looks at the previous owners of this property and possible liens against the property to determine if the current owner really has the right to sell the property. It determines whether there are any outstanding debts that must be settled before the property can be sold.

Liens on property may occur because an owner did not pay back taxes, remodeling or contract charges, or other debts where the courts allowed a lien to be placed. Before you can buy the property, the person who caused this lien must resolve the debt. Homes with this type of problem are said to have *clouds on title*, which means that the title is not free and clear.

For this type of problem, an industry called *title insurance* has been created. Title insurance protects the buyer and lender against loss resulting from claims by others against your home. The title insurance company does the research to determine if the title is free and clear, and then guarantees the result. Most lenders require title insurance.

In many areas, a few days before the closing, the title insurance company will issue a commitment to insure or a *binder* that summarizes any defect on the title and any exceptions from the title insurance coverage. This document goes to the lender and your attorney. If the defects are sizeable or are contrary to what was in the offer contract, this is the point to resolve the problems. If you have an attorney, he or she will review this document and act accordingly.

In some states, attorneys offer the title insurance through a *title insurance company* as part of their service to the homebuyer. The attorney then is the one who deals with the title insurance representative, assists in clearing the title, and provides a title opinion.

Another document that most lenders and title insurance companies insist on is a *land survey.* This marks the boundaries of the property, the structures on it, and any encroachments of the land. Ordering this survey is another service that most real estate attorneys offer the buyers.

HOW TO HOLD TITLE

Joint Tenancy
An attorney can advise you as to how you should hold title to your home. Most couples use *joint tenancy.* Joint tenancy means that the resulting survivor of the two joint tenants owns the property without it going through a will. One of the joint tenants may be able to sell his or her half without the permission of the other, depending on state laws.

Tenancy by the Entireties
Another form of joint tenancy is *tenancy by the entireties,* which is recognized in some states. This is strictly for husband and wife. Besides the benefits of a joint tenancy, tenancy by the entireties prevents one spouse from selling their half without the other spouse's knowledge. It also offers some protection from creditors of one spouse.

Tenancy in Common

The other form of holding title is *tenancy in common*. This is used mostly when the parties do not hold equal shares of the property. In most states, this form of holding *title* is used for commercial property and rental property. It makes for a complex division of the ownership and rights to rental.

chapter thirteen:
The Offer

After thorough research regarding your neighborhood and comparisons of mortgage lenders, you finally find your dream house. It is everything you want or will compromise for, the neighborhood is perfect, and the schools are great. What is the next step?

THE CONTRACT

Next in the home-buying process is to actually make an *offer* on the house. An offer is legally presenting the sellers with a *contract* to purchase and hoping that they will accept it. Because it is a contract for real estate, the offer is made in writing. Real estate agents and brokers have standard forms for their county that are used to communicate the offer.

The buyers fill in this form with the amount offered, the type of mortgage (conventional, VA, FHA), the estimated closing date, and *contingencies*. Contingencies to a contract say that if this event happens, you are not legally liable to buy the house.

Another area in the contract lists what things other than the house and the property are included in the deal. Most times the window coverings and things permanently affixed to the structure or property come with the home. However, each house is different and the laws in your state may allow a very liberal interpretation of what is permanently affixed. If you understand that something is to be sold with the house such as window treatments, appliances, sheds, and such, make sure that these things are listed on your contract offer. This will eliminate confusion on both sides.

Once you sign this contract, you agree to proceed through the deal unless one of the contingencies happen.

ATTORNEY TIP:

Some of the most common contingencies are:
- if the buyer cannot get financing, the seller can cancel the sale;
- if the seller does not provide title to the home, the buyer can cancel the sale; and,
- if the inspector finds insect damage, the buyer can cancel the sale.

WHAT IS IN A REAL ESTATE CONTRACT

Each state and most counties have their own version of what is a *standard residential sales contract*. It may be many paragraphs or something closer to a form with each line numbered. It may have additional agreements that are called *riders,* which are required by local law.

ATTORNEY TIP:

When you start looking for a home, ask your real estate agent for a copy of the standard real estate sale contract for your area. This gives you time to read it and ask questions before the time that you are making the offer.

Because laws on real estate sales differ by state, it is hard to generalize as to what type of contract you will see. Whatever type of document is used, it will be lengthy, have lots of legal phrases, and be overwhelming, especially to first-time homebuyer. It will contain both the buyer's and the seller's name and address, the date of the contract, the address of house being sold, the legal description of the house, a section on financing, a section on inspections, a section listing everything included in the sale, and any contingencies to the sale. There will be places for the buyer, seller, and real estate agents to sign.

Since this is a legal document, you may want a lawyer to represent you before you sign it. An alternative could be to ask that the contract not be effective until your lawyer reviews it. Usually a real estate contract will allow for a short period of time for lawyer review. Most states offer two or three days.

NEGOTIATION

Most times the homebuyer will not want to pay the full price as offered by the sellers. It could be that you feel the home is over priced for the area, there are some problems with the property, or just that you want a bargain. No matter what the reason, most buyers will offer less than the full asking price. *Negotiation* is a process of finding that magic number where both the buyer and seller feel that they are getting a good deal.

In most cases, your real estate agent will help you in this negotiation, but remember, it is in the real estate agent's best interest to make a sale at the highest amount. A real estate attorney can also help you in negotiations.

The real estate agent will help you fill out the proper form and then present it to the seller. In most areas of the country, the buyers put down an amount of *earnest money* (money to show the sellers they are serious about the home) in an *escrow* as a good faith deposit with the offer. The agent will meet with the sellers and/or their agent and *present the offer.* The sellers then have the option to either turn down the offer or make a *counter offer.* This can go on until either the buyer or the seller turns down an offer and does not make a counter.

THINGS TO REMEMBER IN NEGOTIATIONS

- Be firm on the maximum price you are willing to pay for the property, but do not tell your real estate agent. (Do not let the excitement of the negotiations or the pressures of the real estate agent push you beyond that limit.)

- Use the contingency of an inspection to make sure that the house is as sound as has been advertised and that there is no hidden insect damage.
- Use the contingency of being approved for a mortgage by a certain date just in case you cannot get the mortgage you want.
- Know why the sellers are moving and use this information to determine whether they are in a hurry to sell. (For example, if the sellers need to move quickly, they may accept a lower offer just to have the property sold.)
- Do not rush in making an offer. In some areas, houses do sell in one day, this is why you need to know the area. In most cases waiting until you have been able to sleep on it is advisable. (Buyers who rush into an offer can seem very anxious for that house. The sellers may then use that to insist on the full asking price.)

ATTORNEY TIP:

Make tentative plans with your real estate agent to see other homes. This way, your agent gets the idea that your offer is not a life or death decision. The less interest you display, the better your negotiating position.

- Do not limit the options for mortgages. If you qualify for VA or FHA loans, you may want to write one contract for use of one of these and another for use of a conventional loan at a lower price. This way if the seller refuses the VA or FHA loans, you have an immediate counter offer for a conventional loan at a lower purchase price.
- Insist on a twenty-four-hour walk-through the day prior to closing. On occasion, a not-so-ethical seller will remove items, that according to the contract, must be left with the house. (For some sellers this is a game to see how much they can get away with. By insisting

on a walk-through the day prior to the closing, a lot
of this will be eliminated.)
- Play it cool when making the offer. Even though your
insides are churning because you are committing to a
huge debt, avoid showing it to your real estate agent.

EARNEST MONEY

Part of most home purchases is the *earnest money*, which is
held in *escrow* while the parties negotiate. Earnest money is an
amount that indicates that you are a serious buyer. The amount
of earnest money varies from one area to another and is usually paid in cash or a *promissory note*. If the buyer decides to back
out of the deal for a reason which is not a contingency on the
contract, the seller gets the earnest money as payment for their
inconvenience. Of course, the seller and the real estate agent
want a large amount of earnest money.

Escrow

Earnest money is held in what real estate people call *escrow*.
(Also, mortgage companies hold an amount for taxes and home
insurance in escrow.) Escrow is another name for money from
one person that eventually goes to someone else, but is held by
a third person. Some states have licensed escrow agents, some
real estate firms have one person in charge of escrow accounts.

Type 1 Escrow

The buyer puts earnest money into a *Type 1 Escrow* account
when the offer is made. This account contains the earnest
money from the buyer, held by the third party, which will eventually be part of the buyer's payment to the seller. If the offer to
purchase the home is refused, the earnest money is returned to
the buyer. If the offer to purchase the home fails because the
buyer backs out, the seller keeps the money. If the offer to purchase the home fails because of a contingency, the offer contract determines who will keep the money.

Type 2 Escrow

The mortgage company uses a *Type 2 Escrow* account for payments of insurance and taxes. This account contains money the buyer contributes when he or she purchased the house. It is held by the mortgage company until the taxes and insurance bills come due.

chapter fourteen

Appraisers, Inspectors, and Homeowners Insurance

Besides real estate agents and brokers, the second most important real estate professionals you will deal with are the *appraisers*, *inspectors*, and the insurance providers. In most states, these professionals are licensed and/or are required to complete certain educational courses. In areas where there is a lot of real estate activity, the appraisers and inspectors can have appointments months in advance.

Another important person will be your home insurance provider. This person may also send a professional inspector to view your house before providing you with a home insurance policy.

APPRAISERS

The lender usually hires an *appraiser* to make sure that the property is worth the amount of the loan. Some lenders require that the buyer select the appraiser, while others have appraisers on staff or under contract. Your real estate agent or attorney can help you find an appraiser if you need to provide one.

The appraiser's job is to look at the home for obvious defects, look at comparables for other like homes that have sold in the area, and send a report to the mortgage company.

I have dealt with appraisers who spent hours measuring each room, testing each faucet, listening to the furnace, and checking for foundation cracks with a bright light. Others have spent less than fifteen minutes in the house.

What an appraiser looks for is how the sale price (and therefore the loan amount) fits for this type of home in this particular area. If you want to buy a two million-dollar home, in an area where like homes are going for under $50,000, the appraiser is going to ask why.

INSPECTORS

Inspectors usually have more education and experience than appraisers. Besides being trained in certain fields, inspectors can also be specialists, who only do certain types of inspections. Major home inspection associations certify their inspector's credentials. Some of the bigger associations are the *American Society of Home Inspectors (ASHI)* and the *National Association of Home Inspectors (NAHI)*. Your state may also have its own home inspector association.

CLICK ON THIS:

The Internet site www.msn.com 'house and home' section explains in detail many points about home inspections. It has a service that will match inspectors with your zip code.

Specific home inspections are required by the VA and the FHA in order to qualify for the loan. Your offer contract to purchase a house should have a contingent clause in it that requires the house to pass an inspection. Besides your inspection contingency, your mortgage lender and your home insurance provider may also require an inspection. Your real estate agent or attorney may be able to provide you with names of inspectors or you may be able to get a referral from friends, family, or your lender.

The Inspection

Depending upon the inspector, the potential buyer may be able to tag along on the *inspection*. After the inspection is complete, the inspector will write a report and send it to the buyer or his or her attorney for review.

Generally the inspection consists of the following:

- *Drainage.* Rain and snow should drain away from the house to avoid flooding
- *Electrical wiring.* A house may have to be brought up to the local *building code,* if the electrical system is found to be defective or insufficient.
- *Roof.* Leaks in the roof, patches, and multiple layers of roof are important. Leaks can cause damage to interior walls and weaken the structure of the house.

> **ATTORNEY TIP:**
>
> Ask your professional inspector if you can go along on the inspection. Some inspectors have no problem with the potential buyer being there so that defects can be explained, while other inspectors and many sellers prefer that only the inspector who produces a written document do the inspection. If you *do* go along, take your notebook to write down any problems.

- *Furnace and air conditioning.* The age of the furnace and air condition unit is very important. Older furnaces are generally inefficient and can cause outlandish heating bills in addition to wasting energy. There are specific tests, especially for CO_2 gas and other leakage, that will be performed on the furnace.
- *Plumbing.* The inspector will check water pressure and be sure that all faucets and toilets properly operate. He or she will also check for sewage leaks and slow moving drains as an indicator of major problems.
- *Bugs.* Most mortgage companies, including FHA and VA, require a termite inspection. Different areas of the country also include other bugs, since termites can destroy a structure without leaving much evidence. Inspectors or exterminators can perform this test.

- *Ventilation.* The inspector will check windows and doors for leaks and inadequate caulking. The inspector will also check for homes that are so airtight that mold could grow in bathrooms with little ventilation.
- *Foundation.* The foundation will be checked for leaks and cracks.
- *Structural damage.* The entire structure of the building will be checked for damage and indicators that it has been poorly maintained.
- *Environmental.* You can obtain special inspections for radon, lead paint, asbestos, formaldehyde, and other environmental hazards. Certain areas require this type of inspection. (If you have done your research on the neighborhood and found that there was a past leak or other environmental problem in the soil or ground water, you may also want to determine if that environmental problem extended to this property.)

Defects

So what happens when the inspector finds a defect? That answer depends on you and the mortgage company. VA and FHA mortgages require that a house pass a certain level of inspection. Both of these organizations will expect the seller to repair the defect prior to issuing the mortgage.

Conventional lenders can vary in their response to defects. The majority will require that the loan amount be reduced to match the value of the home with the defect. This means that you may have to come up with a larger down payment.

If you have written the offer contract to include the contingency that the home passes an inspection, you can negotiate. Technically, if the home does not pass inspection, you can walk away from the deal. You may have to pay for the inspection, but you should be able to get your escrow money returned.

Another approach is to get the seller to either fix the defect and have the home reinspected or pay you an amount to get the defects repaired. This could be the additional down payment money the lender now requires.

Another plus for the buyer is that in some states the seller must disclose known defects of a serious nature. If the sale goes through and then the buyer finds out about a specific defect, the buyer may be able to sue the seller for funds to repair the property.

INSURANCE

Before you can complete the purchase of your dream house, the mortgage lender will require that you purchase home insurance. You will be required to produce a *Certificate of Insurance, Insurance Binder*, or a document in which the insurance company states that you have insurance on the property at the closing. If you have not obtained insurance by the closing, the closing will stop. You will not be allowed to purchase the home until you obtain insurance.

Home insurance protects the lender's investment and your investment in the property. The mortgage lenders usually require insurance at a certain financial level. In addition, the state in which the property is located may also require that the homeowner get certain types of insurance. If

CLICK ON THIS:

The following sites contain information on homeowners insurance:

www.iii.org
The Insurance Information Institute provides good, basic information on homeowners insurance; how to determine how much insurance you need; where to buy insurance; how to file a claim; and, great tips for lowering your liability.

www.msn.com (house and home)
This site provides information on lowering insurance costs, preventing damage to your house, and links to insurance companies that will give you a quote on homeowners insurance.

www.insweb.com
This site explains the details of homeowners insurance. I feel this is the most informative site on insurance.

While you are at this site, look at Home Insurance Exclusions (things not covered by homeowners insurance). Exclusions talked about range from the common wild animal, water, rats, to the really bizarre occurrences such as religious phenomenon, meteorites, and nuclear irradiation. It is well worth the time to read this section.

the home is located in a flood plain, you will probably be required to obtain flood insurance.

Standard homeowners insurance policies have two sections. The first covers your property and the second covers your liability to be sued for incidents that happen on your property.

The reimbursement for damage to items or to the house itself is usually identified in terms of *actual cash value* and *replacement cost.* Actual cash value takes into consideration depreciation of the item damaged, which would result in the homeowner receiving a reduced amount. Replacement cost is the current dollar amount it takes to replace the property with something of a similar type, which may mean that the insurance company has the right to dictate how your house is repaired.

Homeowners insurance is a complex subject. The mortgage lender, the state, where the house is located, and finally the desires of the homeowner dictate the type of policy and the items covered in the policy.

chapter fifteen:

The Closing

The *closing* or the *settlement* occurs when the buyers, the sellers, the agents, the attorneys, the escrow agent, the title company, the mortgage company, and a host of others sit down to finalize the buy-sell agreement. Many of the people on this list will send a representative *or* a legal document. This is what you have been waiting for—the formal proceeding when that dream house becomes yours.

ATTORNEY TIP:

The day before the closing you should do a walk-through of your soon-to-be new house. This is to determine if there is new damage since the offer and if all the items in the offer contract are still in the home. Your real estate agent should coordinate this.

WHAT REALLY HAPPENS AT A CLOSING

Legally this is the point when the seller transfers the property to the buyer for money. The buyer will be expected to bring certain documents to the closing. The title company or escrow agent will present the buyer and seller with a *settlement statement* that details exact dollar amounts for each part of the sale. The buyer and seller or their attorneys verify the numbers and sign the statement.

Both the seller and the buyer produce *certified checks* for their portion of the closing costs. The buyer then gets to review the mortgage documents, and signs them. The escrow agent, mortgage company, or title agent will establish an escrow account for payment of future property taxes and homeowners insurance. The lender then produces the very large check for the amount of the mortgage loan.

Many other documents are reviewed and signed by both buyer and seller. If appliances or furniture is being sold with the house, a separate document may be required to indicate this. Both buyer and seller then sign the deed. The seller then gives the keys to the buyer.

The final step is done by the escrow agent, title company, or attorney. They will record the newly signed deed with the appropriate city, county, or state office. By recording this deed, the property will be reassessed and the property taxes will probably increase. This is *the* time when you become the owner of your first home.

CLOSING DOCUMENTS

It would be impossible to reproduce the variety of closing documents that real estate professionals use in the United States. Documents vary by type of mortgage, lender, state, county, city, and real estate professionals. The majority of documents are financial ones from your mortgage lender. The following is a minimum list of what you will probably be required to sign. Most real estate transactions end up with about double the number of documents that are listed here.

- The *Real Estate Settlement Procedure Act (RESPA)* requires that the buyer sign a statement to acknowledge that he or she has been informed about how the closing works.
- HUD-1 *Settlement Statement* form itemizes each payment assigned to both the buyer and seller. (See Appendix B.)

- *Truth in Lending Disclosure Statement* will tell the buyer exactly how much it will cost to buy the house. This is the principle amount plus the interest amount.
- *Mortgage Note* or *Contract* is the agreement between the buyer and the mortgage lender to loan the buyer a certain amount. This includes the dates payment is due, interest rates, and other mortgage term information.
- *Security Instrument* (can also be called the *Mortgage* or *Deed*) puts the property up as collateral for the loan.
- *Warranty Deed* transfers the home from the seller to the buyer. In legal terms this then allows the buyer to put the house up as collateral for the mortgage.
- *Escrow papers from the mortgage lender* show the amount of the taxes and insurance escrow.
- *Escrow papers from the earnest money* show the transfer of that amount to the seller.
- *Local tax papers* record the sale to a new homeowner and direct the local taxing authority to send tax bills to your mortgage lender.

What to Bring to the Closing

Your attorney and real estate agent will tell you what to bring to your closing. They may also provide some of the documents. General documents include:

- the offer contract;
- escrow document;
- appraisal;
- inspections;
- property survey;
- title search documents;
- title insurance;
- proof of homeowners insurance;
- proof that the final walk-through was ok; and,
- a certified check for the closing costs.

There may be other documents that are required for your closing depending on the area laws, the type of mortgage, and the standards for sale.

CLOSING COSTS

There are no definitive rules as to who pays for what. Buyers and sellers routinely negotiate closing costs as part of the deal. Even in cases of VA and FHA loans where most closing costs are assigned to the seller, the buyer and seller may make a side deal.

Generally, closing costs consist of the following:
- mortgage application fee;
- points;
- inspections;
- state tax;
- city tax;
- title fees;
- insurance;
- escrow fees;
- document preparation fees; and,
- others.

Amounts vary by size and type of loan, state and local taxes, the total price of the home, and area standards.

ATTORNEY TIP:

Schedule your closing for the afternoon so you will have time in the morning to get a certified check from your bank.

One of the most annoying things about closing costs is that they are difficult to calculate. Only after the lender, the title company, the inspectors, the insurance company, and others do their processing can closing costs be calculated. Usually, the title company is making the calculations about closing costs a day or even hours prior to the actual closing. That does not give the buyer a whole lot of time to get a certified check. This is especially true in areas where there is a lot of real estate activity.

PROBLEMS

There are a few things that can hold up the closing process. Any document that is missing, not filled out right, or does not conform to state real estate laws can stall or even postpone the closing. Expect problems and delays in the closing because it is rare that real estate closings go smoothly, no matter how prepared you are. Even without problems, the closing is guaranteed to last longer than what your real estate agent told you.

An experienced real estate attorney can really help the first-time buyer in the area of the closing and its potential problems. Attorneys that have been through many real estate closings can head off some of the most time-consuming problems by obtaining title searches, mortgage documents, and other required documents for your state—and then reviewing these documents. This type of coordination is especially critical if you are moving into another state or must close the real estate deal on a particular date. A delayed closing can cost both buyer and seller in money and time, and it may even cause the sale to be cancelled. While a real estate attorney is another expense, that attorney can avoid delaying the closing.

The primary action the first-time buyer can take in order to prepare for closing is to gather all the documents that he or she is required to bring. Get a letter from the house insurance company certifying that you have insurance on the building. Bring the exact amount of money, usually cashiers or certified check that you are told to bring. Also bring an amount of cash plus your checkbook for last minute calculation errors. (I would advise withdrawing five hundred to one thousand dollars in cash from your bank account for the closing and then returning what is left to your account that same day.)

If you can, take the entire day off work, so that you will not be concerned with getting back to the job. Also, if you can, don't have the move scheduled for the day of closing. Try to schedule the move a few days after you take possession of the house, which will give you time to clean the interior.

So what do you do if you have a eighteen-wheeler loaded with all your furniture and the closing is postponed? Most movers have temporary storage facilities available if your closing is postponed, but your furniture is already in the moving truck. I have been on the bad end of this type of closing and spent three hours looking for a public storage facility so that the truck could unload. Be smart and ask the movers about this before you sign with them.

Problem closings hit almost everyone. Don't let that diminish your enthusiasm for your new home. Years after the closing, you will be able to laugh about it, honestly. It will give you something to warn your apartment-renting friends about and make good stories for your grandchildren.

SECTION FIVE:
THE FUTURE

chapter sixteen:
Enjoying Your Home

Once you own a home the hard work begins. Besides keeping up with mortgage payments, you will be required to keep up your property. You probably will redecorate, buy furniture, and spend money making this house your home.

ATTORNEY TIP:

The best way to keep up with local information is to subscribe to your local town's newspaper and read it. Certain legal notices such as tax increases, referendums, and other serious changes are usually published in advance to get the residents' input.

RESPONSIBLE HOME OWNERSHIP

It is not enough that you make your mortgage payments. A responsible homeowner is also one who keeps up the property and watches out for problems in the neighborhood before those problems reduce property values. Crime watch is very important nowadays. Your neighborhood may have a group of people who belong to a crime watch organization.

The local police usually sanction organized crime watch groups, so they would be a good source for this information. Some town police departments even offer free services to evaluate your home for break-ins and security. Your local library is also a good source for crime watch information and for copies of your cities local laws. The best thing you can do is to not turn your head when you see a crime or accident. Keep the police phone number by the phone and don't be afraid to report illegal activity.

You may wish to become involved in other town organizations. Some towns have newcomer groups, which are activities for those new to an area. Most towns support volunteer activities that can be socially beneficial and rewarding.

Keeping-up your property is another way to show responsible home ownership. It is not so much a "keeping up with the Joneses" as keeping your property from deteriorating or making a bad appearance. Pick up trash and litter left on your property, even if you did not put it there. Clear leaves, cut the grass, pull weeds, and trim trees. Obtain proper garbage receptacles and replace them when they break.

Be considerate of your neighbors. Mowing the lawn at six am on a Saturday may get the job done, but you will not be the most-liked person on the block. Even though you own the house, remember that the noise of loud parties can be annoying to your neighbors. Be considerate of others.

Also be considerate of parking. If parking is a problem for residents, you may suggest that guests car pool. Also, make sure that guest's cars are not blocking neighbor's driveways or sidewalks. Some towns have laws against parking on the street overnight, after dark, when it snows, or during scheduled street cleaning. Find out what the local laws are in your new town so that you and your guests won't be ticketed.

KEEPING UTILITY EXPENSES DOWN

As a homeowner you will soon discover that utility bills increase almost on a monthly basis. During the winter you get your family to wear sweaters and in the summers you pass around ice, but the utility bills still hurt.

First, look at your furnace and air conditioner. Newer models are more energy efficient and can pay for themselves with lower utility bills.

My home had a fifteen-year-old furnace with central air. In the winter the gas bill was outrageous and in the summer the electricity bill was so bad I was into candlelight dining just to save money. Both units were frequently breaking down. There was one summer when the repairman was out almost every two weeks. In the fall I spoke to my local heating & cooling repair company regarding a quote on replacing both the furnace and central air. Yes, it was a big expense all at once. However, the cost was made up within eighteen months because of reduced utility bills. It really does work.

Another thing you can do to reduce energy bills is to install a programmable thermostat. This allows you to lower the heat when no one is at home and when you sleep; and run the air conditioner on the same type of schedule. These programmable thermostats are available at home repair stores and some department stores. They come with easy to follow instructions and are directed at the do-it-yourselfer.

Furnaces and central air units require certain maintenance. By keeping up with the maintenance the unit will run more efficiently and therefore cost less. Furnaces usually have filters that should be changed according to the directions on the filter or the furnace itself. Following this schedule keeps the air clean and lets the furnace run at its proper level. Also, you should have an annual check on both these appliances by a certified repairperson. This makes sure that the units are running properly and are not leaking noxious fumes. Ask your neighbors for references of qualified technicians.

Another way to save on utility bills is with insulation and caulking. Outside air that comes pouring in around poorly caulked doors and windows can cost money in wasted energy. You may have to replace old, poor fitting windows, or recaulk, or add foam draft strips on the inside of the window. There are

CLICK ON THIS:

For more information on energy savings, check out:

www.consumer.gov

many solutions to this type of problem and some of them are cheap. Go to the local home repair store for more ideas.

As for insulation, you may want to check with your local building code to see what level of insulation is suggested and then make sure the insulation in outside walls and the attic match this level. Your local home repair store will have the supplies and will be able to advise you as to how much insulation is appropriate.

CORRESPONDENCE FROM THE MORTGAGE COMPANY

After you have paid on the mortgage for a while, you may receive a notice that your mortgage has been sold to another lender. This is called the *secondary mortgage market* and it does not mean anything about your creditworthiness is just means you have a new mortgage company. (See Chapter 9 for an explanation on the secondary mortgage market.) The only change you may see is that you will be sending the payment to a new address.

You may also receive a notice that you need to increase the amount of escrow that the mortgage company holds to pay taxes and insurance. This has nothing to do with the escrow that you put down when you made the offer on the house. This is the escrow account that was created at the closing for the purpose of paying taxes and insurance. Because property taxes increase as do insurance premiums, the escrow that was put aside last year may not cover the expenses for this year. This is a legitimate bill, but if you have questions, do not hesitate to contact the new mortgage company.

CONGRATULATIONS— YOU GET A TAX BENEFIT

A person who becomes a homeowner gets a few tax breaks from the IRS. If you paid points when you signed for the mortgage loan, the cost of the points may be deducted in that year's income tax. You can deduct mortgage interest and property tax from your annual income tax. Tax laws may allow additional deductions for the costs of obtaining a mortgage. Plus, if your state has an annual income tax you may get deductions from the state. Certain energy saving devices may also qualify for a tax benefit along with a lower utility bill.

Ask someone who knows the tax laws to do your taxes so that you can take advantage of every deduction available to homeowners. Even though it is one more expense, it is financially worth it to hire an income tax professional to do your annual income tax at least for the first year.

There are some people who want our Congress to remove the deduction for mortgages. So far this has been the one strong deduction that remains without tinkering from the lawmakers or IRS. As a homeowner, you now have a vested interest in keeping this deduction. Even if you are not a political person, pay attention to this issue.

REDUCING YOUR MORTGAGE DEBT

You can reduce the total amount of your mortgage debt by *prepayment.* Any amount of prepayment goes towards the principal amount, not the interest. Therefore you are shortening the length of time it will take to pay off the mortgage. Reductions can mean up to thousands of dollars to you.

ATTORNEY TIP:

When you apply for a mortgage, make sure that it does not have a prepayment penalty. This penalty is charged to keep the homeowner from paying ahead on their mortgage or refinancing at a lower interest rate.

Why would a mortgage company not want you to pay ahead? Interest is how the mortgage company makes money. You do not pay interest on the amount that is paid ahead.

Example:

If you paid an extra $10 per month for a mortgage of $100,000 at 7% interest for thirty years (360 months), it would be paid up in 342 months, and you would save over $8,500.

If you paid an extra $25 per month, the mortgage would be paid up in 320 months at a savings of $18,200 in interest.

The reason prepayment can shorten the life of the mortgage loan goes back to what makes up a mortgage payment: re-payment on the principal, paying the interest, paying taxes, and paying insurance. When mortgages were invented, it was decided to use a calculation called an *amortization table* to decide how much interest and how much principal is paid in each installment.

Generally, payments made early in the mortgage are mostly toward interest, with little toward the principal amount. However, even while the borrower is paying a lot of interest up front, he or she is also slowly paying down the principal debt.

CLICK ON THIS:

To learn more about amortization tables, look at:
- www.interest.com
- www.fha.com
- www.mortgageselect.com
- www.ginniemae.gov
- www.hud.gov
- www.freddiemac.com

chapter seventeen:
Foreclosure and How to Avoid It

Just as many more people are able to afford their own homes—our economy has taken several hard hits. These hits have resulted in thousands losing their jobs and being in real danger of losing their homes as well. The Mortgage Bankers Association recently reported a record number of homeowners who are behind in their mortgage payments and are facing foreclosure.

PREVENTING FORECLOSURE

Preventing a foreclosure begins when you start your search for a home. Borrow only what you can afford. If this means that you must begin with a home that is less than what you really want, then that is what you must do. That is what many people mean when they use the term *starter home*. It is your first home, the one where you build a good credit rating, experience the joys and problems with home ownership, and then sell it to move up to something closer to what you really want.

Many lenders and real estate agents will encourage you to purchase a home that is on the top end of what you can pay for monthly mortgage payments. What these people forget are ongoing expenses like tuition, illness, a new baby, downsizing, or any other expenses that can drain your income. It is up to you to figure these potentials into what you are willing to borrow.

Be careful of the type of mortgage you select. Adjustable rate and balloon mortgages may seem great because in the first years of the mortgage you are paying a lower amount. However, when the rates increase or that balloon payment comes due, you may find yourself unable to make the high payments.

Borrowing against the equity in a home can also cause problems leading to foreclosure. People with multiple mortgages or several home loans against their property can find themselves in a financial problem because they are unable to meet these multiple payments. For every additional mortgage or home loan, you are doubling the risk that you may lose your home.

Along with multiple mortgages are those predatory lenders who like to foreclose on a property because they make more money that way. This usualy happens to people who are cash strapped, the elderly, and those with bad credit ratings. The lender promises to get a person out of debt and then persuade them to take out a high-cost loan that uses the home as collateral.

CLICK ON THIS:

Find out what predatory lending is so that you can avoid it. Look at the following Internet sites for information on this type of fraud:
- www.hud.gov
- www.fdic.gov
- www.stopmortgagefraud.com

You may wish to invest in mortgage insurance in order to pay the mortgage in cases where you cannot. Each policy has its own terms, such as death of the primary income producer in the family, disability, or another severe financial set back. These policies can be expensive at the beginning when the entire mortgage amount is due, but premiums usually lower, the longer the policy is in effect. Your lender

ATTORNEY TIP:

Before signing with any unfamiliar mortgage lender check out the company with the Better Business Bureau, or your state's local consumer protection office.

or insurance agent can probably provide you with information on this type of insurance.

Foreclosure should be avoided at all costs. A foreclosure can cause a problem with a person's credit report for many years. It can cause a person to have major problems whenever they apply for credit cards, car loans, and future mortgages.

WHEN YOU CAN'T PAY THE MORTGAGE

The first thing a homeowner needs to know is that a reputable lender who offers mortgages does not want to foreclose on a home. In addition to the legal costs, there are usually costs associated with getting a building in condition to sell after a foreclosure. The reason is simple—if the homeowner cannot afford the mortgage payment, he or she probably has not been able to pay for maintenance to the home. The key here is a "reputable" lender. Unfortunately, there are some lenders who will prey on the elderly, the inexperienced, and the poor. These lenders eagerly provide a loan at high interest, and when the borrower cannot keep up with the payments quickly move to foreclose and re-sell the home.

What do you do if you find yourself out of a job or faced with bills from a serious illness? This is a two step process—increase money coming in and reduce the expenses. If you have lost your job, you may qualify for unemployment compensation. You may also qualify under your states or Federal assistance plans. Most states have assistance for those without jobs and more local cities are supplementing the state's assistance with their own. Some communities will help with food and utility costs. This assistance can help while you look for a permanent job.

Those who find themselves strapped with large bills from their own or their family's serious illness may also be able to get some assistance from their community or state. If you anticipate large medical bills and you know that you probably will not be able to make payments, notify the hospital or doctor immediately. Waiting until the hospital refers the bills to a collection agency is usually too late. Most collection agencies do not have the ability to negotiate the bill amount. However, many hospitals and clinics employ social workers who can help you get state and local assistance. If you anticipate a problem, be willing to work with that person in resolving your bill.

Assess all of your bills and begin to deal with them one at a time. If you have several high interest credit card bills, you may be able to get that interest rate reduced just by contacting the credit card office. Some loans may allow you to postpone payments for several months if you have lost your job, but do expect to pay extra for this ability.

As for your mortgage, the best thing to do is to contact your lender and see if something can be worked out as soon as the problem arises. Waiting until you have missed several mortgage payments will work against you. If you deal honestly with your mortgage lender, it may be willing to modify your loan or even temporarily suspend payments. Of course, if you have been chronically late in making payments, the lender may not want to work with you.

Lenders hear about money problems all the time. Make sure that your problem is serious and legitimate. Do not attempt to get special consideration from your lender because you want to take a year long vacation or because you want to buy that fancy red sports car. Make sure your financial condition is an emergency.

FEDERAL HOUSING AUTHORITY (FHA), FANNIE MAE, & FREDDIE MAC

In late 2002, these three organizations reported that they had managed to work-out more borrowers in default with loan modifications than ever before. What this means is that these people who were about to lose their homes to foreclosure were able to remain in their homes with some creative financing.

The FHA actually reported that for the first time in sixty years they had paid more to help borrowers retain their homes, than to foreclose.

These companies plus many privately owned lenders are putting programs into place that will help borrowers before the missed payments get so large than the lenders must foreclose on the property. Each case is looked at on an individual basis so we cannot provide any blanket terms that the borrower must follow at this time.

FHA has done the most with a policy of *loan forbearance* especially for those who have temporarily lost their job. *Loan modification* extends the loan for more time while reducing the amount of payment. *Partial claims* are for those who have very high unpaid balances, but are good credit risks. FHA usually leads the mortgage industry in innovations. It is expected that other private lenders will see the benefit of using these same methods.

Staying Positive

Buying a home, especially your first one, is not an easy task. Homebuyers are expected to make major decisions about the future of their finances; about the future of a community; and, about a building that they often have spent less than sixty minutes inside. Through this process, the first-time homebuyer is expected to successfully handle the purchase without the aid of a safety net to catch errors or a crystal ball to predict the future economy.

This book was designed to provide first-time homebuyers with enough knowledge that their fear could be reduced and they could go into the land of real estate without needing a safety net.

A homebuyer who has done research on a community, who has enlisted the help of qualified home inspectors, and who has an understanding of how mortgage financing will work for them can be confident that they have made the right decision when selecting their first home.

The more information that a homebuyer can learn on the process of selecting, financing, and actually purchasing a home, the easier it is for the buyer.

• • • • •

A word to those who bought this book with hopes of getting into their first home right away and for some reason have been forced to put that dream on the back burner.

Do not lose your hopes or your dreams of home ownership. This is the best time to increase your knowledge of the real estate world without the pressure of a purchase right away. Use this time, no matter whether it is one, two, or ten years, to learn about real estate, communities, and government housing. Continue to read the real estate sections in the newspaper. Watch those home shows on TV. Take an occasional "field trip" to another community to look around. Keep increasing your knowledge, even if you think that right now it looks like you will never be able to buy a home. Do not give up on your dream.

With knowledge, you will eventually be able to find that special home that fits both your budget and your lifestyle.

Glossary

A

acceleration clause — part of the mortgage contract that allows the lender to legally demand that the entire mortgage be paid in full because the borrower has failed to make a mortgage payment/s.

adjustable rate mortgage (ARM) — type of mortgage that has a variable interest rate based on a certain percentage or financial interest.

administrator — person who has been appointed by the probate court to dispose of the property owned by someone who has died.

amenity — describes extras provided with a house.

amortization — repayment of the mortgage over a set number of years, which is the term of the mortgage. Lenders will sometimes provide an amortization schedule, which shows the total of each payment and the portion that is put against the principal and the interest amounts.

annual percentage rate (APR) — the cost of a mortgage stated in a yearly term, similar to APRs for cars or credit cards.

annuity — type of insurance policy that will pay a stated amount, usually monthly or annually, to stated recipient.

application — form used to apply for a mortgage that provides information on both the borrower and the property selected.

appraisal — written analysis of the value of a house as prepared by a qualified professional after sufficient inspection. (A lender will use an appraisal to determine the amount it will provide as a mortgage to the homebuyer.)

appraiser — person who is professionally qualified to estimate the value of a property.

appreciation — increase in financial value of a home. (The economy, the neighborhood, the condition of the home, the property the home sits on, and other intangibles influence this value.)

asking price — amount for which a house is offered for sale.

assessed value — value placed on a home by the tax assessor for the purpose of calculating the annual property tax.

assumable mortgage — mortgage contract that can be transferred from one person to another. (Assumable mortgages are desirable when mortgage rates are currently going up and the assumable mortgage has a significantly lower interest rate.)

B

balance sheet — financial statement that shows assets, debts, and net worth.

balloon mortgage — a mortgage contract with low monthly payments that do not increase over time until the final payment. The final payment, due at the end of the term of the mortgage, is usually very large.

bankruptcy — a legal proceeding in federal court in which a person with more debts than assets can reduce the debt under a trustee's direction.

beneficiary — person who receives the proceeds from a trust, will, or estate.

bill of sale — legal document that gives title to personal property. (In a real estate closing, this is used to transfer title to other items that are sold separately by the sellers to the homebuyers.)

binder — term used to indicate a preliminary agreement. (In real estate, a buyer usually provides a binder of earnest money with his/her offer to purchase a home.)

bi-weekly mortgage payments — a mortgage contract that requires the borrower to pay the monthly mortgage amount every two weeks. The mortgage contract itself will dictate how the payments are to be made and the amortization schedule.

building code — local regulations and laws that define all aspects of a structure.

buydown mortgage — a complex way to reduce interest rates and monthly mortgage payments.

buyer's agent — real estate agent hired by the buyer to represent him or her in finding a home and negotiating its purchase.

buyer's remorse — feeling when the buyer realizes that he or she has taken on a large debt.

C

cap — usually refers to a maximum rate of interest or maximum amount of monthly payment on an adjustable rate mortgage (ARM).

capital improvement — a major investment in a home which becomes part of the home, such as remodeled kitchen, dormers, and additional rooms.

certificate of deposit index — index commonly used for interest rate changes in ARM mortgages.

Certificate of Eligibility — used in a VA guaranteed mortgage to prove that the veteran has legally qualified for the loan.

Certificate of Reasonable Value (CRV) — used in a VA guaranteed mortgage, it is the appraisal issued to the Veterans Administration that shows the property's value.

certificate of title — a document drafted by a title company, attorney, or abstract company that states who is the legal owner of a property.

chain of title — the history of who owned or had liens on property.

Chamber of Commerce — association of merchants for the promotion of commercial interests in the community; provide valuable information on the town.

clear title — a title to property which does not have liens or legal complications.

closing — the event where the purchase of the property is completed. It is usually attended by the buyer, seller, and lender (or their legal representatives). Documents are signed, money exchanged, and the buyer gets the keys to the home.

closing costs — expenses in addition to the price of the property that are paid by both buyer and seller.

closing statement — document commonly called a HUD1 (the number on the form) that lists the final costs incurred to get the mortgage loan and buy the home.

cloud on title — a lien on a title that must be cleared up for the title to pass from the seller to the buyer.

collateral — an asset put up to guarantee that a loan will be repaid. (In a mortgage, the property is put up as collateral.)

commission — in real estate transactions, the percentage of the sale price that the seller pays to his or her real estate agent.

commitment letter — promise from a lender to provide the borrower with a mortgage.

comparables — similar properties in the same area that have recently sold.

contingency — a condition that must be met before a contract can be enforced. (In an offer contract for real estate, common contingencies are that the property pass inspections and the buyers are able to obtain financing.)

contract sale or deed — document between the buyer and seller that conveys the title to the property.

conventional loan — mortgage that is not insured by FHA or VA.

convertible ARM — an adjustable rate mortgage that can be converted to a fixed-rate mortgage on certain conditions.

Cost of Funds Index (COFI) — an index that may be used to set interest rates in an ARM.

cost of living — cost of the basic necessities of life.

counter offer — home seller's response to buyer's offer on the house.

credit report — a professionally created report on a person's credit history.

credit scores — a number which represents the likelihood that a person will pay their bills on time that is calculated by the credit bureaus. *See FICO.*

D

debt-to-income ratio — the percentage of a person's income that is already allocated to debts such as, mortgages, loans, utilities, and credit cards.

deed — legal document that conveys title to a property.

deed of trust — in some states this legal document is used in place of, or in addition to, a mortgage document to secure the payment.

default — when a person does not pay on the mortgage or any loan, they are considered in default of the loan.

deferred interest — a mortgage that is written so the interest payments are delayed for a time.

delinquency — another word for default. Failure to make payments on a loan or mortgage.

Department of Housing and Urban Development (HUD) — government agency whose primary purpose is to provide mortgage insurance.

Department of Veterans Affairs (VA) — agency of the U.S. government that manages benefits and other issues for veterans of the military.

depreciation — the decline in value of a property; opposite of appreciation.

direct lender — a mortgage lender of any size that makes loans from the lenders' own portfolio of assets.

discount points — *See points.*

down payment — the amount of initial money a buyer will pay for a property in addition to the money from a mortgage.

due-on-sale clause — legal clause in the mortgage contract that allows the lender to demand immediate payment of the balance on the mortgage when the mortgage holder sells the home.

E

earnest money — a significant amount of money that the potential buyer puts down with the offer to buy that shows that the potential buyer is serious about going through with the deal.

easement — right of way given to someone other than the owner of a property that allows some access to the property. (Some examples are a shared driveway, a common fence, and utility poles.)

eminent domain — the right of government to take private property for public use after the property owner is paid market value for the property.

encroachment — an improvement that illegally intrudes on someone else's property.

encumbrance — something that limits the ownership of a property, such as mortgage, liens, or easements.

Equal Credit Opportunity Act (ECOA) — federal law that requires lenders to make credit equally available for all people without discrimination as to race, color, religion, natural origin, age, sex, marital status, or receiving income from public assistance programs.

equity — the amount of financial interest an owner has in his or her property.

escrow — in purchasing real estate, a third party holds earnest money in escrow. The third party will deliver the escrow amount upon certain conditions, such as the purchase of the property.

escrow account — the term used by mortgage companies for the funds used to pay the tax on a property. (When the property taxes are increased, the mortgage company will require that the owner add more to this fund.)

examination of title — taking the ownership of property from the initial sale to the current date using public records.

exclusive listing — a contract between the seller and real estate agent for a specified time that allows the agent to market the property, assist in the sale, and obtain a commission.

F

Fair Credit Reporting Act — law that protects consumers through federal regulations on the total interest paid over the life of the loan and procedures to repair errors on a person's credit report.

fair market value — the current price at which a property should sell.

Fannie Mae or Federal National Mortgage Association (FNMA) — a corporation created by the government that buys and sells conventional mortgages and mortgages that are insured by the FHA or VA.

Farmers Home Administration (FmHA) — organization that provides loans specifically to farmers who are unable to find other financing.

Federal Home Loan Mortgage Corporation or Freddie Mac (FHLMC) — agency that purchases conventional mortgages from HUD approved bankers.

Federal Housing Administration (FHA) — division of HUD that insures residential mortgage loans and sets standards for underwriting.

Federal National Mortgage Association (FNMA) or Fannie Mae — a corporation created by the government that buys and sells conventional mortgages and mortgages that are insured by the FHA or VA.

Federal Trade Commission (FTC) — government agency that monitors credit bureaus.

FHA loan — loan insured by the Federal Housing Administration.

FICO — a credit score calculation, developed by Fair Isaac & Co., that private credit bureaus use to indicate the likelihood that a person will pay his or her bills on time.

firm commitment — lender's agreement to provide a mortgage loan.

fixed rate mortgages — mortgage where the interest and the payment remain the same for the term of the loan.

fixture — personal property that becomes part of the real estate such as a shed attached to the garage or curtain rods bolted to the wall.

flood insurance — insurance for losses due to water damage. (This may be required by the lender.)

foreclosure — legal process where a lender forces the sale of property because the borrower could not make the mortgage payments.

401(k) — employer-sponsored investment program to set aside tax-deferred money for retirement.

Freddie Mac or Federal Home Loan Mortgage Corporation (FHLMC) — agency that purchases conventional mortgages from HUD approved bankers.

G

Ginnie Mae or Government National Mortgage Association (GNMA) — agency of the government that purchases conventional mortgages from HUD approved bankers.

Government National Mortgage Association (GNMA) or Ginnie Mae — agency of the government that purchases conventional mortgages from HUD approved bankers.

grantee — person who gets the property (buyer).

grantor — person who gives the property (seller).

gross monthly income — income received each month from every source before taxes and before deductions for employer incentive savings program (401k).

guaranty — promise to pay the debts of another.

H

handy-man's special — term with no set definition by the real estate industry; usually refers to a home that needs maintenance.

hazard insurance — insurance against specific losses.

home inspection — done by a professional to evaluate structural and mechanical condition of a property.

home warranty — insures a new home against major structural damage for a set period of time, usually ten years.

homeowners association — a group of owners who manage the common areas and set the rules. Usually found in condominiums or closed communities.

homeowner's insurance — insurance policy that protects the owners and the mortgage holder from loss.

house value — determined by upkeep of the home, upgrades made to the home, the neighborhood, and the economy.

I

impound — that portion of the monthly mortgage payment that is held in escrow by the lender to pay for taxes and insurance.

income property — property such as an apartment building, a condominium, or a house which is rented out for money.

index — a rate used to compute the index on adjustable rate mortgages.

inflation — increase in the general price level of goods and services.

informational sheet — piece of paper real estate agents possess containing the details of a home.

inspector — person hired to complete a thorough examination of the house on behalf of the buyer; credentials certified by major home inspection associations.

installment loan — loan that is repaid in equal payments over a particular time period, such as a mortgage or car loan.

insurable title — title to a property for which a title insurance company has agreed to issue a policy.

insurance binder — a document written by an insurance company that states that temporary insurance is in effect. (This is required at a closing to prove that the buyer has contacted the insurance company and they will provide insurance coverage.)

interest — the cost for borrowing money.

J

joint tenancy — ownership of a property by two or more people. Each person holds an undivided part of the property. (For example, a husband and wife can each own 50% of property in joint tenancy.)

judgment — legal decision issued by a court. (In real estate, it is used to place liens against a property for non-payment of debts or taxes.)

judicial foreclosure — type of foreclosure used in many states that is conducted under the supervision of a court.

jurisdiction — the area where the property is located.

L

late charge — financial penalty for making a debt payment past the due date. Some lenders will charge a financial penalty in addition to adding a mark on your credit report.

lease-purchase mortgage loans — *See rent with an option to buy.*

legal description — description of the property that is what is recorded in public records. (A professional surveyor usually does this.)

lender — bank or financial institution that lends money to buyers.

lien — a legal claim against the property that must be cleared before the owner can sell the property.

liquid assets — those things that can quickly be converted to cash. (Stocks and bonds are types of examples.)

listing agent — the real estate agent who signs the contract with the seller to *list* the property for sale. This can also be the seller's or buyer's agent in the transaction.

loan forbearance — *See loan modification.*

loan modification — extends the loan for more time while reducing the amount of payment.

loan origination — procedures that a lender follows to produce a mortgage on real property.

lock-in — a written contract from the lender that guarantees a particular interest rate on a particular property for a set period of time.

M

market value — approximate price that a property can get when sold. (It is calculated by looking at comparables and factoring in the potential growth of the area.)

mechanic's lien — lien placed against property by an "unpaid" private contractor.

mortgage — a loan for purchase of property where the property is put up as collateral.

mortgage banker — company that exclusively writes mortgages to buyers and sells mortgages to other mortgage bankers.

mortgage broker — a person who finds a mortgage for a buyer for a fee or commission.

mortgagee — the lender.

mortgage insurance — an insurance contract that will pay the lender should the borrower default on the mortgage loan.

mortgage life insurance — insurance policy that will pay the rest of the mortgage due if the primary borrower dies.

mortgagor — the borrower.

Multiple Listing Services (MLS) — provides information to all real estate agents that are registered members about every house that other members are selling.

N

net worth — value of all the person's assets minus all his or her debts.

note — legal document that obligates a borrower to repay a debt.

notice of default — legal written document that informs the borrower that he or she is considered in default due to lack of payment on a loan and that legal proceedings will follow.

O

offer — legally presenting the seller(s) with a contract to purchase; acceptance is not guaranteed.

origination fee — *See points.*

owner financing — seller provides part or all of the financing in the sale of real estate.

P

payment history — part of a person's credit report; records of late and on-time payments.

points — an amount paid to the lender for processing the mortgage. It is measured in terms of points, with one point equal to one percent of the mortgage amount.

portfolio lenders — a mortgage lender who makes loans from the lender's own portfolio of assets.

power of attorney — legal document that allows a person to act for another in a legal transaction. (In some real estate sales, the seller will give his or her agent the power of attorney to stand in for the seller at the closing.)

pre-approval — agreement from a lender to loan a buyer a particular amount of money.

prearranged financing agreement — used in some areas of the country to prove that the buyer has been pre-approved for a mortgage loan.

prepayment — payment made in addition to the required monthly mortgage payment. (Prepayment allows a borrower to pay down a mortgage loan quicker than originally planned as the payment goes against the principal, not the interest.)

prepayment penalty — charge for paying ahead on a mortgage.

pre-qualified — buyer who has been preliminarily approved for a loan. This is not a guarantee and will depend on further investigation.

principal — amount of debt on a loan that does not include interest.

principal, interest, taxes, and insurance (PITI) — components of a monthly mortgage payment.

private mortgage insurance (PMI) — agreement to give money to the lender if the buyer defaults on his or her payments.

promissory note — legal agreement to repay a certain amount of money.

property tax — tax against the owner of real estate; deductible from annual federal income tax filing.

public auction — process whereby property that has been foreclosed is sold.

purchase and sale agreement — legal document signed by both the buyer and seller to pass property for a certain amount of money and with specific terms.

Q

quit claim deed — a deed that transfers property without warranty. The seller transfers whatever interest he/she has in the property at that point in time to the buyer, without warranting that the seller has any interest at all.

R

radon — radioactive gas found in some homes that may or may not cause health problems.

real estate agent — person who is licensed to process the sale of real estate.

real estate broker — person who does the same duties as a real estate agent, in addition to specific home searches, arranging funding, and negotiating contracts.

real estate laws — regulations on a city, county, or state level that direct real estate transactions and the actions of real estate agents/brokers.

Real Estate Settlement Procedures Act (RESPA) — law that provides consumer protection by requiring lenders to give borrowers notice of closing costs.

real property — legal name for the home, the land, other permanent structures, and all other rights included as the property for sale.

realtor® — real estate professional who has membership in a local real estate board that is affiliated with the *National Association of Realtors.*

recission — cancellation of a transaction or contract.

recorder — public official or office who legally records the deed after the property has been sold or transferred.

refinance — exchanging an old mortgage for a new mortgage with a lower interest rate.

rent with an option to buy — agreement between the owner of property and the potential buyer whereby the rent or a portion of the rent will be applied to a down payment on the property at a certain date.

rider — additional clause(s) in a real estate contract that are required by local law.

right of ingress or egress — in real estate, it is the right to enter or leave a portion of the property.

right of survivorship — characteristic of joint tenancy. If one of the owners dies, the other owner gets the deceased's portion without going through a will.

S

secondary market — the purchase of existing mortgages by other lenders. (This usually does not increase mortgage payments, but can effect the benefits offered with the mortgage loan.)

secured loan — loan that is backed by collateral.

seller's agent — the real estate agent who represents the seller of the property in the transaction.

settlement — another name for the closing.

settlement statement — form used at closing or settlement. (Commonly referred to as the HUD-1 statement.)

starter home — beginning home that is less that what the buyer really wants for purposes of building credit and experience in home ownership.

survey — measurement of the land by a registered surveyor. It produces the legal description of the property with references to known points, dimensions, buildings, and natural items (trees, rocks, and streams).

T

tenancy by the entirety — type of joint tenancy available to married couples. It includes the right of survivorship and protection from one spouse selling the home without the permission of the other.

tenancy in common — way to hold title of property where the owners do not have to hold equal shares and do not have the right of survivorship.

term — period of months or years needed to payback a mortgage.

title — document that proves a person's ownership of a property.

title insurance — insurance policy that protects the homebuyer from errors in the title search if those errors cause financial loss.

title search — check of records of who owned the property and what liens have been placed on the property from the time the property was built.

total expense ratio — person's debts as a percentage of his or her gross income, usually calculated on a monthly basis.

transfer of ownership — action whereby ownership of a property changes hands.

transfer tax — state and/or city tax on the sale of a home.

treasury index — one type of index used in ARMs based on auctions held by the U.S. Treasury for Bills and Securities.

truth in lending — federal law that requires the lender to disclose all financial aspects of a mortgage in writing.

Type 1 Escrow — account that contains earnest money from the buyer, held by a third party, which will eventually be part of the buyer's payment to the seller.

Type 2 Escrow — account used for payments of insurance and taxes.

U

underwriting — the process of evaluating and investigating a loan application.

unsecured loan — a loan not backed by collateral.

V

VA mortgage — mortgage that is guaranteed by the Department of Veterans Affairs.

vested — usually used to indicate the percentage of ownership an employee has in his/her retirement account.

Veterans Affairs, Department of (VA) — agency of the U.S. government which manages benefits and other issues for veterans of the military.

W

Welcome Wagon — a person or group that provides information and gifts from local merchants to new residents; can be a useful source of information on a particular town.

wraparound mortgage — an additional mortgage that includes payments on prior mortgages.

appendix a:
State Offices
of Real Estate Regulation

Following is a list of the state governmental agencies that regulate real estate professionals. This may include agents, brokers, inspectors, and appraisers. Each state issues its own license to the real estate professionals who work there. The requirements for such a license varies from state to state.

The information on the Internet sites listed range from things that just help the real estate professional renew their license, to sites that provide help for the home buyer. The majority of sites list the laws that the real estate professional must follow, and the education required for a license. Many list the names of state licensed real estate professionals and offer a way to make a complaint against one of these people. Check the Internet site for the state you want to buy a home in. It may provide you with some information on selecting your real estate professional.

- **Alabama Real Estate Commission**
  www.arec.state.al.us
  334-242-5544

- **Alaska Real Estate Commission**
  www.dced.state.ak.us/occ/prec.htm
  907-269-8160

- **Arizona Department of Real Estate**
  www.re.state.az.us
  602-468-1414

- **Arkansas Real Estate Commission**
  www.state.ar.us/arec/
  501-683-8010

- **California Real Estate Licensing Board**
  www.dre.ca.gov

- **Colorado Division of Real Estate**
  www.dora.state.co.us/real-estate/
  303-894-2166

- **Connecticut Licensing Department**
  www.dcp.state.ct.us/licensing/realestate.htm
  860-566-3290

- **Delaware Real Estate Commission**
  www.professionallicensing.state.de.us/boards
  /realestate/index.shtml
  302-739-4522

- **District of Columbia Department of Consumer and Regulatory Affairs**
  202-727-7450

- **Florida Department of Business & Professional Regulation**
  www.state.fl.us/dbpr/re/dre.shtml
  407-245-0800

- **Georgia Real Estate Commission**
  www.state.ga.us/Ga.Real_Estate/
  404-656-3916

- **Hawaii Real Estate Commission**
  www.state.hi.us/hirec
  808-586-2643

- **Idaho Real Estate Commission**
  www.idahorealestatecommission.com
  208-334-3285

- **Illinois Office of Banks and Real Estate**
  www.obre.state.il.us
  312-782-3000 or 217-782-3000

- **Indiana Real Estate Commission**
www.in.gov/pla/bandc/estate
317-232-2980

- **Iowa Real Estate Commission**
www.state.ia.us
515-281-3183

- **Kansas Real Estate Commission**
www.accesskansas.org/krec/
785-296-3411

- **Kentucky Real Estate Commission**
www.krec.net
502-425-4273

- **Louisiana Real Estate Commission**
www.lrec.state.la.us
800-821-4529

- **Maine Office of Licensing**
www.state.me.us/pfr/olr/
207-624-8603

- **Maryland Real Estate Commission**
www.dllr.state.md.us/license/occprof/recomm.html
410-230-6200

- **Massachusetts Real Estate Board**
www.mass.gov
617-727-2373

- **Michigan Office of Commercial Services**
www.michigan.gov/cis/
517-241-9288

- **Minnesota Real Estate Comission**
www.state.mn.us
651-296-6319

- **Mississippi Real Estate Commission**
www.mrec.state.ms.us
601-932-9191

- **Missouri Real Estate Commission**
  www.ded.state.mo.us
  573-751-2628

- **Montana Board of Realty Regulation**
  www.discoveringmontana.com/dli/bsd/
  406-444-2961

- **Nebraska Real Estate Commission**
  www.nrec.state.ne.us
  402-471-2004

- **Nevada Real Estate Division**
  www.red.state.nv.us
  775-687-4280 or 702-486-4033

- **New Hampshire Real Estate Commission**
  www.state.nh.us/nhrec/
  603-271-2701

- **New Jersey Department of Real Estate Licensing**
  www.nj.gov/dobi/rec_lic.htm
  609-292-8280

- **New Mexico Real Estate Commission**
  www.nmrealtor.com/2001site/nmrec_frame.htm
  505-841-9120 or 800-801-7505

- **New York Department of State
  Division of Licensing Services**
  www.dos.state.ny.us/lcns/realest.html
  518-473-2728

- **North Carolina Real Estate Commission**
  www.ncrec.state.nc.us
  919-875-3700

- **North Dakota Real Estate Commission**
  www.governor.state.nd.us
  701-328-9749 or 701-328-9737

- **Ohio Real Estate and
  Professional Licensing Division**
  www.com.state.oh.us/real/
  614-466-4100

- **Oklahoma Real Estate Commission**
  www.orec.state.ok.us
  800-448-4904

- **Oregon Real Estate Agency**
  www.rea.state.or.us
  503-378-4170

- **Pennsylvania Real Estate Commission**
  www.dos.state.pa.us/bpoa/cwp
  717-783-4854

- **Rhode Island Department of Business Regulation**
  www.dbr.state.ri.us/real_estate.html
  401-222-2355

- **South Carolina Real Estate Commission**
  www.llr.state.sc.us/POL/RealEstateCommission/
  803-896-4400

- **South Dakota Real Estate Commission**
  www.state.sd.us/dcr/realestate/
  605-773-3600

- **Tennessee Real Estate Commission**
  www.state.tn.us/commerce/trec/
  800-342-4031

- **Texas Real Estate Commission**
  www.trec.state.tx.us
  512-459-6544

- **Utah Division of Real Estate**
  www.commerce.utah.gov/dre/
  801-530-6747

- **Vermont Real Estate Commission**
  www.vtprofessionals.org/
  802-828-3228

- **Virginia Department of Professional
  and Occupational Regulation**
  www.state.va.us/dpor.indexne.html
  804-367-8500

- **Washington Department of Professional Licensing**
  www.dol.wa.gov/realestate
  360-586-6101

- **West Virginia Real Estate Commission**
  www.state.wv.us/wvrec/
  304-558-3555

- **Wisconsin Real Estate Licensing Board**
  www.drl.state.wi.us
  608-266-5511

- **Wyoming Real Estate Commission**
  www.realestate.state.wy.us
  307-777-7141

appendix b:
HUD-1 Settlement Statement

When the real estate agent/broker, attorney, or title company tells you the total amount of the certified check that you must bring to the closing, you may wonder how they arrived at that number. Even those of us who have experience in buying and selling homes have problems understanding how they come up with a total amount. In order to resolve this universal question the HUD-1 Settlement Statement was created. It is used to list in detail the costs paid by both the buyer and seller. Besides being an explanation of what you are paying for, this form is also a checklist for those in the title company who are preparing the closing documents to make sure that all costs are covered and that missing costs will not delay the closing. The buyer and seller should use this form to quickly verify, at the closing, that they are not being erroneously charged for something.

This is a sample of a document that is required in every house sale. It breaks down the costs for both buyer and seller at the time of the sale.

A. **Settlement Statement**

U.S. Department of Housing
and Urban Development

OMB Approval No. 2502-0265

B. Type of Loan

1. ☐ FHA 2. ☐ FmHA 3. ☐ Conv. Unins.	6. File Number:
4. ☐ VA 5. ☐ Conv. Ins.	7. Loan Number:
	8. Mortgage Insurance Case Number:

C. Note: This form is furnished to give you a statement of actual settlement costs. Amounts paid to and by the settlement agent are shown. Items marked "(p.o.c.)" were paid outside the closing; they are shown here for informational purposes and are not included in the totals.

D. Name & Address of Borrower:	E. Name & Address of Seller:	F. Name & Address of Lender:

G. Property Location:	H. Settlement Agent:
	Place of Settlement:
	I. Settlement Date:

J. Summary of Borrower's Transaction		K. Summary of Seller's Transaction	
100. Gross Amount Due From Borrower		**400. Gross Amount Due To Seller**	
101. Contract sales price		401. Contract sales price	
102. Personal property		402. Personal property	
103. Settlement charges to borrower (line 1400)		403.	
104.		404.	
105.		405.	
Adjustments for items paid by seller in advance		Adjustments for items paid by seller in advance	
106. City/town taxes to		406. City/town taxes to	
107. County taxes to		407. County taxes to	
108. Assessments to		408. Assessments to	
109.		409.	
110.		410.	
111.		411.	
112.		412.	
120. Gross Amount Due From Borrower		**420. Gross Amount Due To Seller**	
200. Amounts Paid By Or In Behalf Of Borrower		**500. Reductions In Amount Due To Seller**	
201. Deposit or earnest money		501. Excess deposit (see instructions)	
202. Principal amount of new loan(s)		502. Settlement charges to seller (line 1400)	
203. Existing loan(s) taken subject to		503. Existing loan(s) taken subject to	
204.		504. Payoff of first mortgage loan	
205.		505. Payoff of second mortgage loan	
206.		506.	
207.		507.	
208.		508.	
209.		509.	
Adjustments for items unpaid by seller		Adjustments for items unpaid by seller	
210. City/town taxes to		510. City/town taxes to	
211. County taxes to		511. County taxes to	
212. Assessments to		512. Assessments to	
213.		513.	
214.		514.	
215.		515.	
216.		516.	
217.		517.	
218.		518.	
219.		519.	
220. Total Paid By/For Borrower		**520. Total Reduction Amount Due Seller**	
300. Cash At Settlement From/To Borrower		**600. Cash At Settlement To/From Seller**	
301. Gross Amount due from borrower (line 120)		601. Gross amount due to seller (line 420)	
302. Less amounts paid by/for borrower (line 220)	(	602. Less reductions in amt. due seller (line 520)	( )
303. Cash ☐ From ☐ To Borrower		**603. Cash** ☐ To ☐ From Seller	

Section 5 of the Real Estate Settlement Procedures Act (RESPA) requires the following: • HUD must develop a Special Information Booklet to help persons borrowing money to finance the purchase of residential real estate to better understand the nature and costs of real estate settlement services; • Each lender must provide the booklet to all applicants from whom it receives or for whom it prepares a written application to borrow money to finance the purchase of residential real estate; • Lenders must prepare and distribute with the Booklet a Good Faith Estimate of the settlement costs that the borrower is likely to incur in connection with the settlement. These disclosures are manadatory.

Section 4(a) of RESPA mandates that HUD develop and prescribe this standard form to be used at the time of loan settlement to provide full disclosure of all charges imposed upon the borrower and seller. These are third party disclosures that are designed to provide the borrower with pertinent information during the settlement process in order to be a better shopper.

The Public Reporting Burden for this collection of information is estimated to average one hour per response, including the time for reviewing instructions, searching existing data sources, gathering and maintaining the data needed, and completing and reviewing the collection of information.

This agency may not collect this information, and you are not required to complete this form, unless it displays a currently valid OMB control number.

The information requested does not lend itself to confidentiality.

L. Settlement Charges

	Paid From Borrowers Funds at Settlement	Paid From Seller's Funds at Settlement
700. **Total Sales/Broker's Commission based on price $ @ % =**		
Division of Commission (line 700) as follows:		
701. $ to		
702. $ to		
703. Commission paid at Settlement		
704.		
800. Items Payable In Connection With Loan		
801. Loan Origination Fee %		
802. Loan Discount %		
803. Appraisal Fee to		
804. Credit Report to		
805. Lender's Inspection Fee		
806. Mortgage Insurance Application Fee to		
807. Assumption Fee		
808.		
809.		
810.		
811.		
900. Items Required By Lender To Be Paid In Advance		
901. Interest from to @ $ /day		
902. Mortgage Insurance Premium for months to		
903. Hazard Insurance Premium for years to		
904. years to		
905.		
1000. Reserves Deposited With Lender		
1001. Hazard insurance months @ $ per month		
1002. Mortgage insurance months @ $ per month		
1003. City property taxes months @ $ per month		
1004. County property taxes months @ $ per month		
1005. Annual assessments months @ $ per month		
1006. months @ $ per month		
1007. months @ $ per month		
1008. months @ $ per month		
1100. Title Charges		
1101. Settlement or closing fee to		
1102. Abstract or title search to		
1103. Title examination to		
1104. Title insurance binder to		
1105. Document preparation to		
1106. Notary fees to		
1107. Attorney's fees to		
(includes above items numbers:)		
1108. Title insurance to		
(includes above items numbers:)		
1109. Lender's coverage $		
1110. Owner's coverage $		
1111.		
1112.		
1113.		
1200. Government Recording and Transfer Charges		
1201. Recording fees: Deed $; Mortgage $; Releases $		
1202. City/county tax/stamps: Deed $; Mortgage $		
1203. State tax/stamps: Deed $; Mortgage $		
1204.		
1205.		
1300. Additional Settlement Charges		
1301. Survey to		
1302. Pest inspection to		
1303.		
1304.		
1305.		
1400. Total Settlement Charges (enter on lines 103, Section J and 502, Section K)		

appendix c:
Internet Sites by Subject

SUBJECT	INTERNET SITE
Affordability calculator	www.ginniemae.gov
Amortization tables	www.fha.com
	www.freddiemac.com
	www.ginniemae.gov
	www.hud.gov
	www.interest.com
	www.mortgageselect.com
Buy vs. Rent info	www.ginniemae.gov
Closing Costs Calculator	www.freddiemac.com
Closing information	www.ginniemae.gov
Credit Bureau Reports	www.equifax.com
	www.experian.com
	www.tuc.com
Debt-to-Income Ratio	www.fha.com
Decorating	www.hgtv.com
Discrimination in housing	www.hud.gov
	www.ginniemae.gov
Down Payment Calculator	www.freddiemac.com
Energy Savings	www.comsumer.gov

SUBJECT	INTERNET SITE
Fannie Mae / Federal National Mortgage Association	www.fanniemae.com
FHA / Federal Housing Admin.	www.fha.com
FICO/credit scores	www.yourmortgage.net
	www.myfico.com
Find a home for sale by area	www.realtor.com
Find a real estate agent by area	www.realtor.com
Find a home for sale by area	www.msn.com (house & home)
Fraud in mortgages	www.stopmortgagefraud.com
Freddie Mac	www.freddiemac.com
General info	www.fha.com
	www.ginniemae.gov
	www.hud.gov
	www.interest.com
	www.msn.com (house & home)
Ginnie Mae / Government National Mortgage Association	www.ginniemae.gov
Home buying road map	www.msn.com (house & home)
Home Repairs	www.hgtv.com
Housing & Urban Development (HUD)	www.hud.gov
Inspections	www.msn.com (house & home)
	www.ginniemae.gov
Insurance	www.iii.org
	www.insweb.com
	www.msn.com (house & home)

SUBJECT	INTERNET SITE
Mortgage Calculators	www.ginniemae.gov
	www.hud.gov
	www.interest.com
	www.mortgageselect.com
	www.hgtv.com
	www.ourownhome.net
	www.fanniemae.com
	www.msn.com
	(house & home)
Mortgage term glossary	www.ourownhome.net
Mortgage Types	www.fha.com
	www.interest.com
Neighborhood Research	www.msn.com
	(house & home)
Predatory Lending / Fraud	www.fdic.gov
	www.stopmortgagefraud.com
	www.hud.gov
Rehabbing	www.hgtv.com
Taxes	www.freddiemac.com
Veteran's mortgage assistance	www.va.gov

appendix d:
Worksheets

Worksheet 1:   **What I want In My Neighborhood** is used to list all the things that are important to a person about a neighborhood and then priortize those items.

Worksheet 2:   **Features I Want In My Home** is a four page worksheet used to rank features that a person wants in their future home.

Worksheet 3:   **Viewing A House For Sale** is a two page worksheet to be used when looking at a house that is up for sale. It has places for notes and sizes for both interior and exterior.

Worksheet 4:   **Comparing Mortgage Lenders** is a two page worksheet to be used when comparing four different lenders and the loans that they are offering.

WORKSHEET 1:
WHAT I WANT IN MY NEIGHBORHOOD

STEP 1—Write down all those things that are important to you in a neighborhood - don't mix ideas on the same line. (Ex: Close to certain church, near recreation, in walking distance for schools, etc.)

WHAT I WANT	RANK

STEP 2 -- Now go back and rank each item by how important it is to you, with number 1 being most important.

STEP 3 -- After you have ranked you entire list, go back and put an asterisk * next to the rank number of those items you absolutely MUST HAVE. Try to limit you MUST HAVES to five.

STEP 4 -- Compare your list with that of the other person you are buying the house with.

WORKSHEET 2:
FEATURES I WANT IN MY HOME

Price Range: from $_____ to $_____

Type/Style of Building: _____

Wheelchair Access: ___   Special Needs: _____

No. of Bedrooms Must Have: _____

No. of Bathrooms Must Have: _____

FEATURES	IMPORTANCE RANK (1 Most—5 Least)				
	1	2	3	4	5
Large yard (1 acre or more)					
Fenced yard					
Outside patio or deck					
In ground pool					
Professionally landscaped					
Fenced dog run					
Carport					
Garage—No. of cars _____					
Garage attached to house					
Other outside buildings					
Well & septic					
City water & sewer					
Personal water source					
Forced air gas furnace					

FEATURES	IMPORTANCE RANK (1 Most—5 Least)				
	1	2	3	4	5
Baseboard / Radiator heat					
Heat pump					
Central air conditioner					
KITCHEN:					
Eat in					
Appliances remain					
Work island					
New or recently remodeled					
BEDROOMS:					
Master bedroom					
Private bath in master bedroom					
Bedroom on main level					
Sitting room					
Family room					
Great Room					
Den					
Library					
Basement					

FEATURES	IMPORTANCE RANK (1 Most—5 Least)				
	1	2	3	4	5
Laundry room					
Home office					
Computer connections throughout					
Formal living room					
Formal dining room					
Hardwood floors					
Wall to wall carpeting					
Fireplace—In what rooms:					
In-law apartment					
Other Features:					

FEATURES	IMPORTANCE RANK (1 Most—5 Least)				
	1	2	3	4	5

WORKSHEET 3:
VIEWING A HOUSE FOR SALE

Date you saw house: _____

Realtor_____

_____

Asking price: $_____

Taxes: $_____Water source: City _____ Well _____

Address: _____

_____

Description: _____

_____

_____

_____

Lot size: _____   House sqare footage: _____

Age: _____

<u>INTERIOR:</u>

ROOM	SIZE	NOTES
Kitchen		
Laundry area		
Basement		
Living Room		
Dining Room		
Den		
Great-room		
Master Bedroom		
Bedroom 2		
Bedroom 3		
Bedroom 4		
Bedroom 5		
Bathroom 1		
Bathroom 2		
Bathroom 3		
Bathroom 4		

Appliances and other furniture sold with house:

_____

_____

_____

_____

_____

_____

_____

_____

Heat type: _____

Air conditioning type: _____

EXTERIOR:

Surface of house: _____

_____

Gutters: _____

Deck, patio, outside porch: _____

Garage: _____

Parking: _____

_____

NOTES:

_____

_____

_____

_____

_____

_____

_____

_____

_____

_____

_____

WORKSHEET 4:
COMPARING MORTGAGE LENDERS

MORTGAGE AMOUNT: $ _____

LENDER #1:

Name: _____

Contact: _____

Address: _____

_____

Phone/e-mail:

_____

LENDER #2:

Name: _____

Contact: _____

Address: _____

_____

Phone/e-mail:

_____

LENDER #3:

Name: _____

Contact: _____

Address: _____

_____

Phone/e-mail:

_____

LENDER #4:

Name: _____

Contact: _____

Address: _____

_____

Phone/e-mail:

_____

	#1	#2	#3	#4
Loan type (fixed rate, adjustable, VA, FHA, other				
Down payment required				
Length of loan				
Annual Percentage Rate				
Points				
Estimated escrow				
Estimated monthly payment inTotal				
Application / loan processing fee				
Origination / underwriting fee				
Lender fee / funding fee				
Appraisal fee				
Document preparation & recording fee				
Points				
Credit report fee				
Other fees charged by lender				
Prepayment available				
Cost of letter to lock in mortgage rate				

NOTES:

_____

_____

_____

_____

_____

_____

_____

_____

_____

_____

_____

_____

_____

_____

_____

appendix e:
VA Guaranteed Loan

The following sample forms will prepare you for the specific information required to apply for a VA Loan. As stated in Chapter 11, if you are considering applying for this type of a loan, be sure to consult a real estate professional and/or an attorney who practices in this specific real estate matter. The application is complicated, but worth the effort if you are eligible.

INSTRUCTIONS FOR PREPARATION OF VA REQUEST FOR DETERMINATION OF REASONABLE VALUE

RESPONDENT BURDEN: VA may not conduct or sponsor, and respondent is not required to respond to this collect information unless it displays a valid OMB Control Number. Public reporting burden for this collection of information is est: to average 12 minutes per response, including the time for reviewing instructions, searching existing data sources, gatherir maintaining the data needed, and completing and reviewing the collection of information. If you have comments regardir burden estimate or any other aspect of this collection of information, call 1-800-827-1000 for mailing information on where to send your comments.

NOTE: ALL ENTRIES MUST BE TYPED

Remove this instruction page and complete page 1 following the instructions below, using the reverse of this instruction pag worksheet. After completion of page 1, detach page 2 for your records and forward the packet, together with any necessary e: to the VA office having jurisdiction.

Since certain selected data from page 1 is transcribed onto the VA CRV (Certificate of Reasonable Value), we request that thi be carefully prepared. Incomplete submissions impede timely processing at the expense of both the Government and the requeste

This report is authorized by law (38 U.S.C. 3704(a) and 3710(b). Failure to provide the information requested can result in rej of the property as security for a loan.

REQUIRED EXHIBITS TO BE SENT WITH APPLICATION

SALES CONTRACTS: In cases involving proposed construction or existing construction not previously occupied, a copy executed or proposed sales contract must be submitted or, if a previously approved form of contract is to be used, the app contract code number may be shown in Item 37. In those cases in which a veteran is under contract, submission of the contrac be deferred until a loan application is received.

PROPOSED CONSTRUCTION: Complete working drawings, including plot plan, foundation or basement plans, plans of all exterior elevations, grade levels, sectional wall details, heating layout, individual well and septic system layout, and specificatic VA Form 26-1852, Description of Materials. (Consult local VA office for number of exhibit sets required.) This informa subject to reproduction by VA under 38 U.S.C. 3705 (b) and for storage purposes.

EXISTING CONSTRUCTION: 1. ALTERATIONS, IMPROVEMENTS OR REPAIRS - Complete drawings and specific indicating the work to be done and its relation to the house, in the quantity required by the local VA office. 2. NOT PREVIO OCCUPIED AND CONSTRUCTION COMPLETED WITHIN 12 CALENDAR MONTHS - Contact local VA office for elig criteria and required exhibits.

FORM ENTRIES

NAME, ADDRESS, AND ZIP CODE: Make sure to enter the ZIP code in all blocks which require an address entry.

LEGAL DESCRIPTION: Insert legal description. If necessary, attach 4 copies of a separate sheet showing the legal description.

TITLE LIMITATIONS: Enter known title exceptions. If none are known, enter "None." Include easements, special assessments, mandatory homeowners association membership, etc. Exceptions noted on this application will be considered in reasonable value. Attach separate sheet (4 copies) if necessary.

LOT DIMENSIONS: Show frontage X depth. If irregular, indicate dimensions of all perimeter lot lines.

REMOVABLE EQUIPMENT: Personal property, such as furniture, drapes and rugs, will not be valued and may not be included in the loan. However, wall-to-wall carpeting may be included in value and also included in the loan.

CONSTRUCTION COMPLETED: Insert both month and year when property has been completed less than two years. If over two years old, insert year completed only.

COMMENTS ON SPECIAL ASSESSMENTS AN HOMEOWNER ASSOCIATION CHARGES: Indicate s assessments which are now a lien or will become a lien. case of a planned unit development, condominium, mandatory membership homeowner association, indicat current monthly or other periodic assessment.

MINERAL RIGHTS: If reserved, explain either in space s as title exceptions or by separate page.

LEASEHOLD CASES: (Usually Hawaii or Marylanc property involves a leasehold, insert the ground rent pe and show whether the lease is for 99 years or renew whether it has previously been VA approved, and its expi date. Submit two copies of the lease agreement.

SALE PRICE: Enter proposed sale price except application involves an individual owner-occupant buildir himself/herself. In such cases, enter estimated co construction and the balance owned on the lot, if ar refinancing, enter amount of proposed loan in Item 35.

NOTE: If title is not "fee simple," submit copies in duplicate of all pertinent legal data providing a full explanation of the title involved.

OMB APPROVED NO. 2900-0045
RESPONDENT BURDEN: 12 minutes

REQUEST FOR DETERMINATION OF REASONABLE VALUE (Real Estate)

1. CASE NUMBER	4. TITLE LIMITATIONS AND RESTRICTIVE COVENANTS:

2. PROPERTY ADDRESS (Include ZIP Code and county)	3. LEGAL DESCRIPTION

1. ☐ CONDOMINIUM   2. ☐ PLANNED UNIT DEVELOPMENT

6. LOT DIMENSIONS:

1. ☐ IRREGULAR: SQ/FT   2. ☐ ACRES:

5. NAME AND ADDRESS OF FIRM OR PERSON MAKING REQUEST/APPLICATION (Include ZIP Code)

7. UTILITIES (✓)	ELEC.	GAS	WATER	SAN. SEWER
1. PUBLIC				
2. COMMUNITY				
3. INDIVIDUAL				

8. EQUIPMENT		
1. ☐ RANGE/OVEN	4. ☐ CLOTHES WASHER	7. ☐ VENT FAN
2. ☐ REFRIG.	5. ☐ DRYER	8. ☐ W/W CARPET
3. ☐ DISH WASHER	6. ☐ GARBAGE DISPOSAL	9.

9. BUILDING STATUS	10. BUILDING TYPE	11. FACTORY FABRICATED?	12A. NO. OF BUILDINGS	12B. NO. OF LIVING UNITS	13A. STREET ACCESS	13B. STREET MAINTENANCE
1. ☐ PROPOSED 3. ☐ EXISTING 2. ☐ UNDER CONSTRUCTION 4. ☐ ALTERATIONS, IMPROVEMENTS, OR REPAIRS	1. ☐ DETACHED 3. ☐ ROW 2. ☐ SEMI-DETACHED 4. ☐ APT UNIT	1. ☐ YES 2. ☐ NO			1. ☐ PRIVATE 2. ☐ PUBLIC	1. ☐ PRIVATE 2. ☐ PUBLIC

14A. CONSTRUCTION WARRANTY INCLUDED?	14B. NAME OF WARRANTY PROGRAM	14C. EXPIRATION DATE (Month, day, year)	15. CONSTRUCTION COMPLETED (Mo.,yr.)
1. ☐ YES 2. ☐ NO (If "Yes," complete Items 14b and 14c also)			

16. NAME OF OWNER	17. PROPERTY: ☐ OCCUPIED BY OWNER ☐ NEVER OCCUPIED ☐ VACANT ☐ OCCUPIED BY TENANT (Complete Item 18 also)	18. RENT (If applic.) $ / MONTH

19. NAME OF OCCUPANT	20. TELEPHONE NO.	21. NAME OF BROKER	22. TELEPHONE NO.	23. DATE AND TIME AVAILABLE FOR INSPECTION ☐ AM ☐ PM

24. KEYS AT (Address)	25. ORIGINATOR'S IDENT. NO.	26. SPONSOR'S IDENT. NO.	27. INSTITUTION'S CASE NO.

28. PURCHASER'S NAME AND ADDRESS (Complete mailing address, Include ZIP Code)

EQUAL OPPORTUNITY IN HOUSING

NOTE: Federal laws and regulations prohibit discrimination because of race, color, religion, sex, or national origin in the sale or rental of residential property. Numerous State statutes and local ordinances also prohibit such discrimination. In addition, section 805 of the Civil Rights Act of 1968 prohibits discriminatory practices in connection with the financing of housing.

If VA finds there is noncompliance with any antidiscrimination laws or regulations, it may discontinue business with the violator.

29. NEW OR PROPOSED CONSTRUCTION - Complete Items 29A through 29G for new or proposed construction cases only

A. COMPLIANCE INSPECTIONS WILL BE OR WERE MADE BY: ☐ FHA ☐ VA ☐ NONE MADE	B. PLANS (Check one) ☐ FIRST SUBMISSION ☐ REPEAT CASE (If checked complete Item 29C)	C. PLANS SUBMITTED PREVIOUSLY UNDER CASE NO.
D. NAME AND ADDRESS OF BUILDER	E. TELEPHONE NO.	F. NAME AND ADDRESS OF WARRANTOR	G. TELEPHONE NO.

30. COMMENTS ON SPECIAL ASSESSMENTS OR HOMEOWNERS ASSOCIATION CHARGES	31. ANNUAL REAL ESTATE TAXES $	33. LEASEHOLD CASES (Complete if applicable)
	32. MINERAL RIGHTS RESERVED? ☐ YES (Explain) ☐ NO	A. LEASE IS: ☐ 99 YEARS ☐ RENEWABLE	B. EXPIRES (Date)	C. ANNUAL GROUND RENT $

34A. SALE PRICE OF PROPERTY $	34B. IS BUYER PURCHASING LOT SEPARATELY? ☐ YES ☐ NO (If "Yes," see instruction page under "Sale Price")	35. REFINANCING-AMOUNT OF PROPOSED LOAN $	36. PROPOSED SALE CONTRACT ATTACHED ☐ YES ☐ NO	37. CONTRACT NO. PREVIOUSLY APPROVED BY VA THAT WILL BE

CERTIFICATIONS FOR SUBMISSIONS TO VA

1. On receipt of "Certificate of Reasonable Value" or advice from the Department of Veterans Affairs that a "Certificate of Reasonable Value" will not be issued, we agree to forward to the appraiser the approved fee which we are holding for this purpose.

2. CERTIFICATION REQUIRED ON CONSTRUCTION UNDER FHA SUPERVISION (Strike out inappropriate phrases in parentheses)

I hereby certify that plans and specifications and related exhibits, including acceptable FHA Change Orders, if any, supplied to VA in this case, are identical to those (submitted to) (to be submitted to) (approved by) FHA inspections, and that FHA inspections (have been) (will be) made pursuant to FHA approval for mortgage insurance on this basis of proposed construction under Sec.

38. SIGNATURE OF PERSON AUTHORIZING THIS	39. TITLE	40. TELEPHONE NUMBER	41. DATE

42. DATE OF ASSIGNMENT	43. NAME OF APPRAISER

WARNING: Section 1010 of title 18, U.S.C. provides: "Whoever for the purpose of...influencing such Administration...makes, passes, utters or publishes any statement knowing the same to be false...shall be fined not more than $5,000 or imprisoned not more than two years or both."

VA FORM JUN 2001   **26-1805**   SUPERSEDES VA FORM 26-1805, DEC 1992, WHICH WILL NOT BE USED.   **VA FILE COPY 1**

OMB APPROVED NO. 2900-0045
RESPONDENT BURDEN: 12 minutes

REQUEST FOR DETERMINATION OF REASONABLE VALUE (Real Estate)

1. CASE NUMBER	4. TITLE LIMITATIONS AND RESTRICTIVE COVENANTS:

2. PROPERTY ADDRESS (Include ZIP Code and county)	3. LEGAL DESCRIPTION

	1. CONDOMINIUM	2. PLANNED UNIT DEVELOPMENT

5. NAME AND ADDRESS OF FIRM OR PERSON MAKING REQUEST/APPLICATION (Include ZIP Code)	6. LOT DIMENSIONS:

1. IRREGULAR: SQ/FT   2. ACRES:

7. UTILITIES (✓)	ELEC.	GAS	WATER	SAN. SEWER
1. PUBLIC				
2. COMMUNITY				
3. INDIVIDUAL				

8. EQUIP.	1.	RANGE/OVEN	4.	CLOTHES WASHER	7.	VENT FAN
	2.	REFRIG.	5.	DRYER	8.	W/W CARPET
	3.	DISH WASHER	6.	GARBAGE DISPOSAL	9.	

9. BUILDING STATUS	10. BUILDING TYPE	11. FACTORY FABRICATED?	12A. NO. OF BUILDINGS	12B. NO. OF LIVING UNITS	13A. STREET ACCESS	13B. STREET MAINTENANCE
1. PROPOSED 3. EXISTING ALTERATIONS, IMPROVEMENTS, 2. UNDER CONSTRUCTION 4. OR REPAIRS	1. DETACHED 3. ROW APT. 2. SEMI-DETACHED 4. UNIT	1. YES 2. NO			1. PRIVATE 2. PUBLIC	1. PRIVATE 2. PUBLIC

14A. CONSTRUCTION WARRANTY INCLUDED?	14B. NAME OF WARRANTY PROGRAM	14C. EXPIRATION DATE (Month, day, year)	15. CONSTRUCTION COMPLETED (Mo.,yr.)
1. YES 2. NO (If "Yes," complete Items 14b and 14c also)			

16. NAME OF OWNER	17. PROPERTY:		18. RENT (If applic.)
	OCCUPIED BY OWNER NEVER OCCUPIED VACANT	OCCUPIED BY TENANT (Complete Item 18 also)	$ / MONTH

19. NAME OF OCCUPANT	20. TELEPHONE NO.	21. NAME OF BROKER	22. TELEPHONE NO.	23. DATE AND TIME AVAILABLE FOR INSPECTION
				AM PM

24. KEYS AT (Address)	25. ORIGINATOR'S IDENT. NO.	26. SPONSOR'S IDENT. NO.	27. INSTITUTION'S CASE NO.

28. PURCHASER'S NAME AND ADDRESS (Complete mailing address. Include ZIP Code)	EQUAL OPPORTUNITY IN HOUSING

EQUAL OPPORTUNITY IN HOUSING NOTE: Federal laws and regulations prohibit discrimination because of race, color, religion, sex, or national origin in the sale or rental of residential property. Numerous State statutes and local ordinances also prohibit such discrimination. In addition, section 805 of the Civil Rights Act of 1968 prohibits discriminatory practices in connection with the financing of housing.

If VA finds there is noncompliance with any antidiscrimination laws or regulations, it may discontinue business with the violator.

29. NEW OR PROPOSED CONSTRUCTION - Complete Items 29A through 29G for new or proposed construction cases only

A. COMPLIANCE INSPECTIONS WILL BE OR WERE MADE BY:	B. PLANS (Check one)	C. PLANS SUBMITTED PREVIOUSLY UNDER CASE NO.
FHA VA NONE MADE	FIRST SUBMISSION REPEAT CASE (If checked complete Item 29C)	

D. NAME AND ADDRESS OF BUILDER	E. TELEPHONE NO.	F. NAME AND ADDRESS OF WARRANTOR	G. TELEPHONE NO.

30. COMMENTS ON SPECIAL ASSESSMENTS OR HOMEOWNERS ASSOCIATION CHARGES	31. ANNUAL REAL ESTATE TAXES $	33. LEASEHOLD CASES (Complete if applicable)	
	32. MINERAL RIGHTS RESERVED? YES (Explain) NO	A. LEASE IS: 99 YEARS RENEWABLE	B. EXPIRES (Date)
			C. ANNUAL GROUND RENT $

34A. SALE PRICE OF PROPERTY	34B. IS BUYER PURCHASING LOT SEPARATELY?	35. REFINANCING-AMOUNT OF PROPOSED LOAN	36. PROPOSED SALE CONTRACT ATTACHED	37. CONTRACT NO. PREVIOUSLY APPROVED BY VA THAT WILL BE
$	(If "Yes," see instruction page under "Sale Price") YES NO	$	YES NO	

CERTIFICATIONS FOR SUBMISSIONS TO VA

1. On receipt of "Certificate of Reasonable Value" or advice from the Department of Veterans Affairs that a "Certificate of Reasonable Value" will not be issued, we agree to forward to the appraiser the approved fee which we are holding for this purpose.

2. CERTIFICATION REQUIRED ON CONSTRUCTION UNDER FHA SUPERVISION (Strike out inappropriate phrases in parentheses)

I hereby certify that plans and specifications and related exhibits, including acceptable FHA Change Orders, if any, supplied to VA in this case, are identical to those (submitted to) (to be submitted to) (approved by) FHA inspections, and that FHA inspections (have been) (will be) made pursuant to FHA approval for mortgage insurance on this basis of proposed construction under Sec.

38. SIGNATURE OF PERSON AUTHORIZING THIS	39. TITLE	40. TELEPHONE NUMBER	41. DATE

42. DATE OF ASSIGNMENT	43. NAME OF APPRAISER

WARNING: Section 1010 of title 18, U.S.C. provides: "Whoever for the purpose of . . .influencing such Administration . . .makes, passes, utters or publishes any statement knowing the same to be false . . .shall be fined not more than $5,000 or imprisoned not more than two years or both.

VA FORM JUN 2001   **26-1805**   SUPERSEDES VA FORM 26-1805, DEC 1992, WHICH WILL NOT BE USED.   **VA FILE COPY 1**

OMB APPROVED NO. 2900-0045
RESPONDENT BURDEN: 12 minutes

REQUEST FOR DETERMINATION OF REASONABLE VALUE (Real Estate)

1. CASE NUMBER	4. TITLE LIMITATIONS AND RESTRICTIVE COVENANTS:

2. PROPERTY ADDRESS (Include ZIP Code and county)	3. LEGAL DESCRIPTION	

1. ☐ CONDOMINIUM   2. ☐ PLANNED UNIT DEVELOPMENT

5. NAME AND ADDRESS OF FIRM OR PERSON MAKING REQUEST/APPLICATION (Include ZIP Code)	6. LOT DIMENSIONS:

1. ☐ IRREGULAR: SQ/FT   2. ☐ ACRES:

7. UTILITIES (✓)	ELEC.	GAS	WATER	SAN. SEWER
1. PUBLIC				
2. COMMUNITY				
3. INDIVIDUAL				

8. E
Q 1. ☐ RANGE/OVEN   4. ☐ CLOTHES WASHER   7. ☐ VENT FAN
U 2. ☐ REFRIG.   5. ☐ DRYER   8. ☐ W/W CARPET
I
P. B. ☐ DISH WASHER   6. ☐ GARBAGE DISPOSAL   9. ☐

9. BUILDING STATUS		3. ☐ EXISTING	10. BUILDING TYPE	11. FACTORY FABRICATED?	12A. NO. OF BUILDINGS	12B. NO. OF LIVING UNITS	13A. STREET ACCESS	13B. STREET MAINTENANCE
1. ☐ PROPOSED	ALTERATIONS, IMPROVEMENTS, OR REPAIRS		1. ☐ DETACHED 3. ☐ ROW				1. ☐ PRIVATE	1. ☐ PRIVATE
2. ☐ UNDER CONSTRUCTION 4. ☐			2. ☐ SEMI-DETACHED 4. ☐ APT UNIT	1. ☐ YES 2. ☐ NO			2. ☐ PUBLIC	2. ☐ PUBLIC

14A. CONSTRUCTION WARRANTY INCLUDED?	14B. NAME OF WARRANTY PROGRAM	14C. EXPIRATION DATE (Month, day, year)	15. CONSTRUCTION COMPLETED (Mo.,yr.)
1. ☐ YES 2. ☐ NO (If "Yes," complete Items 14b and 14c also)			

16. NAME OF OWNER	17. PROPERTY:	18. RENT (If applic.)
	☐ OCCUPIED BY OWNER ☐ NEVER OCCUPIED ☐ VACANT ☐ OCCUPIED BY TENANT (Complete Item18 also)	$ / MONTH

19. NAME OF OCCUPANT	20. TELEPHONE NO.	21. NAME OF BROKER	22. TELEPHONE NO.	23. DATE AND TIME AVAILABLE FOR INSPECTION ☐ AM ☐ PM

24. KEYS AT (Address)	25. ORIGINATOR'S IDENT. NO.	26. SPONSOR'S IDENT. NO.	27. INSTITUTION'S CASE NO.

28. PURCHASER'S NAME AND ADDRESS (Complete mailing address, Include ZIP Code)	EQUAL OPPORTUNITY IN HOUSING

EQUAL OPPORTUNITY IN HOUSING
NOTE: Federal laws and regulations prohibit discrimination because of race, color, religion, sex, or national origin in the sale or rental of residential property. Numerous State statutes and local ordinances also prohibit such discrimination. In addition, section 805 of the Civil Rights Act of 1968 prohibits discriminatory practices in connection with the financing of housing.

If VA finds there is noncompliance with any antidiscrimination laws or regulations, it may discontinue business with the violator.

29. NEW OR PROPOSED CONSTRUCTION - Complete Items 29A through 29G for new or proposed construction cases only

A. COMPLIANCE INSPECTIONS WILL BE OR WERE MADE BY:	B. PLANS (Check one)	C. PLANS SUBMITTED PREVIOUSLY UNDER CASE NO.
☐ FHA ☐ VA ☐ NONE MADE	☐ FIRST SUBMISSION ☐ REPEAT CASE (If checked complete Item 29C)	

D. NAME AND ADDRESS OF BUILDER	E. TELEPHONE NO.	F. NAME AND ADDRESS OF WARRANTOR	G. TELEPHONE NO.

30. COMMENTS ON SPECIAL ASSESSMENTS OR HOMEOWNERS ASSOCIATION CHARGES	31. ANNUAL REAL ESTATE TAXES $	33. LEASEHOLD CASES (Complete if applicable)	
	32. MINERAL RIGHTS RESERVED? ☐ YES (Explain) ☐ NO	A. LEASE IS: ☐ 99 YEARS ☐ RENEWABLE	B. EXPIRES (Date) C. ANNUAL GROUND RENT $

34A. SALE PRICE OF PROPERTY	34B. IS BUYER PURCHASING LOT SEPARATELY?	35. REFINANCING-AMOUNT OF PROPOSED LOAN	36. PROPOSED SALE CONTRACT ATTACHED	37. CONTRACT NO. PREVIOUSLY APPROVED BY VA THAT WILL BE
$	(If "Yes," see Instruction page under "Sale Price") ☐ YES ☐ NO	$	☐ YES ☐ NO	

CERTIFICATIONS FOR SUBMISSIONS TO VA

1. On receipt of "Certificate of Reasonable Value" or advice from the Department of Veterans Affairs that a "Certificate of Reasonable Value" will not be issued, we agree to forward to the appraiser the approved fee which we are holding for this purpose.

2. CERTIFICATION REQUIRED ON CONSTRUCTION UNDER FHA SUPERVISION (Strike out inappropriate phrases in parentheses)

I hereby certify that plans and specifications and related exhibits, including acceptable FHA Change Orders, if any, supplied to VA in this case, are identical to those (submitted to) (to be submitted to) (approved by) FHA inspections, and that FHA inspections (have been) (will be) made pursuant to FHA approval for mortgage insurance on this basis of proposed construction under Sec.

38. SIGNATURE OF PERSON AUTHORIZING THIS	39. TITLE	40. TELEPHONE NUMBER	41. DATE

42. DATE OF ASSIGNMENT	43. NAME OF APPRAISER

WARNING: Section 1010 of title 18, U.S.C. provides: "Whoever for the purpose of . . .influencing such Administration . . .makes, passes, utters or publishes any statement knowing the same to be false . . .shall be fined not more than $5,000 or imprisoned not more than two years or both.

VA FORM JUN 2001   **26-1805**   SUPERSEDES VA FORM 26-1805, DEC 1992, WHICH WILL NOT BE USED.   **REQUESTOR'S COPY 2**

OMB APPROVED NO. 2900-0045
RESPONDENT BURDEN: 12 minutes

CERTIFICATE OF REASONABLE VALUE

1. CASE NUMBER	4. TITLE LIMITATIONS AND RESTRICTIVE COVENANTS·

2. PROPERTY ADDRESS (Include ZIP Code and county)	3. LEGAL DESCRIPTION	

1. ☐ CONDOMINIUM   2. ☐ PLANNED UNIT DEVELOPMENT

5. NAME AND ADDRESS OF FIRM OR PERSON MAKING REQUEST/APPLICATION (Include ZIP Code)	6. REMAINING ECONOMIC LIFE OF PROPERTY IS ESTIMATED TO BE NOT LESS THAN (Enter number of years)

YEARS

7. ESTIMATED REASONABLE VALUE OF PROPERTY	8. EXPIRATION DATE

$

9. SECRETARY OF VETERANS AFFAIRS BY (Signature of authorized agent)

10. DATE ISSUED	11. VA OFFICE

GENERAL CONDITIONS

(NOTE: THE DEPARTMENT OF VETERANS AFFAIRS DOES NOT ASSUME ANY RESPONSIBILITY FOR THE CONDITION OF THE PROPERTY. THE CORRECTION OF ANY DEFECTS NOW EXISTING OR THAT MAY DEVELOP WILL BE THE RESPONSIBILITY OF THE PURCHASER.)

1. This certificate will remain effective as to any written contract of sale entered into by an eligible veteran within the validity period indicated.
2. This dwelling conforms with the Minimum Property Requirements prescribed by the Secretary of Veterans Affairs.
3. The aggregate of any loan secured by this property plus the amount of any assessment consequent on any special improvements as to which a lien or right to a lien shall exist against the property, except as provided in Item 13 below, may not exceed the reasonable value in Item 7 above.
4. Proposed construction shall be completed in accordance with the plans and specifications identified below, relating to both onsite and offsite improvements upon which this valuation is based and shall otherwise conform fully to the VA Minium Property Requirements. Satisfactory completion must be evidenced by either:
   A. VA Final Compliance Inspection Report (VA Form 26-1839), or
   B. VA Acceptance of FHA Compliance Inspection Reports or other evidence of completion under FHA supervision applicable to proposed construction.
5. By contracting to sell property, as proposed construction or existing construction not previously occupied, to a veteran purchaser who is to be assisted in the purchase by a loan made, guaranteed, or insured by VA, the builder or other seller agrees to place any downpayment received by the seller or agent of the seller in a special trust account as required by section 3706 of title 38, U.S. Code.
6. The VA guaranty is subject to and conditioned upon the lending institution's compliance, at the time of the making, increasing, extending or renewing of the proposed loan, with section 102 of P.L. 93-234, "Flood Disaster Protection Act of 1973."

12. PURCHASER'S NAME AND ADDRESS (Complete mailing address, Include ZIP Code)	13. EXCEPTIONS TO GENERAL CONDITION NO. 3 ABOVE

☐ ENERGY EFFICIENT MORTGAGE PROGRAM - The buyer may wish to contact a qualified person/firm for a home energy audit to identify needed energy efficiency improvements to the property. In some localities, the utility company may perform this service. The mortgage amount may be increased as a result of making energy efficiency improvements such as: Solar or conventional heating/cooling systems, water heaters, insulation, weather-stripping/caulking, and storm windows/doors. Other energy related improvements may also be considered. The mortgage may be increased by (a) up to $3,000 based solely on documented costs; or, (b) up to $6,000 provided the increase in monthly mortgage payment does not exceed the likely reduction in monthly utility costs; or, (c) more than $6000 subject to a value determination by VA.
☐ OTHER (Cite and explain in Item 26 below)

SPECIFIC CONDITIONS (Applicable when checked or completed)

14. THE REASONABLE VALUE ESTABLISHED HEREIN FOR THE RELATED PROPERTY IS:	15. PROPOSED CONSTRUCTION TO BE COMPLETED

☐ BASED UPON OBSERVATION OF THE PROPERTY IN ITS "AS IS" CONDITION
☐ PREDICATED UPON COMPLETION OF PROPOSED CONSTRUCTION (If checked, complete Item 15)
☐ PREDICATED UPON COMPLETION OF REPAIRS LISTED IN ITEM 17

16. INSPECTIONS REQUIRED	17. REPAIRS TO BE COMPLETED

☐ FHA COMPLIANCE INSPECTIONS FOR PROPOSED CONSTRUCTION
☐ VA COMPLIANCE INSPECITONS   ☐ LENDER TO CERTIFY

18. NAME OF COMPLIANCE INSPECTOR

19. HEALTH AUTHORITY APPROVAL - Execution of Health Authority form or letter indicating approval of the individual:	20.

☐ WATER SUPPLY   ☐ SEWAGE DISPOSAL SYSTEM

This document is subject to the provisions of Executive Orders 11246 and 11375, and the Rules and Regulations of the Secretary of Labor in effect on this date, and 38 CFR 36.4390 through 36.4393, and also the provisions of the certification ☐ executed by the builder, sponsor or developer named herein which is on file in this office.

21. ☐ WOOD DESTROYING INSECT INFORMATION - EXISTING CONSTRUCTION - The seller shall, at no cost to the veteran-purchaser, prior to settlement, obtain a written statement from a qualified pest control operator reporting wood destroying insect information using the NPCA-1, National Pest Control Association form or other form acceptable to VA.

22. WARRANTY	23. NAME OF WARRANTOR	24.

☐ (If checked, complete item 23)

☐ Since this property is located in a Special Flood Hazard Area as established by FEMA, flood insurance will be required in accordance with 38 CFR 36.4326

25. SAFE DRINKING WATER ACT

☐ Certification required that in construction, any solders and flux did not contain more than 0.2 percent lead and any pipes and pipe fittings did not contain more than 8.0 percent lead.

26. OTHER REQUIREMENTS

VA FORM JUN 2001 **26-1843**	SUPERSEDES VA FORM 26-1805, DEC 1992, WHICH WILL NOT BE USED.	REQUESTOR'S COPY 3

OMB APPROVED NO. 2900-0045
RESPONDENT BURDEN: 12 minutes

CERTIFICATE OF REASONABLE VALUE

1. CASE NUMBER	4. TITLE LIMITATIONS AND RESTRICTIVE COVENANTS:

2. PROPERTY ADDRESS (Include ZIP Code and county)	3. LEGAL DESCRIPTION	

1. ☐ CONDOMINIUM   2. ☐ PLANNED UNIT DEVELOPMENT

5. NAME AND ADDRESS OF FIRM OR PERSON MAKING REQUEST/APPLICATION (Include ZIP Code)	6. REMAINING ECONOMIC LIFE OF PROPERTY IS ESTIMATED TO BE NOT LESS THAN (Enter number of years) YEARS

7. ESTIMATED REASONABLE VALUE OF PROPERTY $	8. EXPIRATION DATE

9. SECRETARY OF VETERANS AFFAIRS BY (Signature of authorized agent)

10. DATE ISSUED	11. VA OFFICE

GENERAL CONDITIONS

(NOTE: THE DEPARTMENT OF VETERANS AFFAIRS DOES NOT ASSUME ANY RESPONSIBILITY FOR THE CONDITION OF THE PROPERTY. THE CORRECTION OF ANY DEFECTS NOW EXISTING OR THAT MAY DEVELOP WILL BE THE RESPONSIBILITY OF THE PURCHASER.)

1. This certificate will remain effective as to any written contract of sale entered into by an eligible veteran within the validity period indicated.

2. This dwelling conforms with the Minimum Property Requirements prescribed by the Secretary of Veterans Affairs.

3. The aggregate of any loan secured by this property plus the amount of any assessment consequent on any special improvements as to which a lien or right to a lien shall exist against the property, except as provided in Item 13. below, may not exceed the reasonable value in Item 7 above.

4. Proposed construction shall be completed in accordance with the plans and specifications identified below, relating to both onsite and offsite improvements upon which this valuation is based and shall otherwise conform fully to the VA Minimum Property Requirements. Satisfactory completion must be evidenced by either:
   A. VA Final Compliance Inspection Report (VA Form 26-1839), or
   B. VA Acceptance of FHA Compliance Inspection Reports or other evidence of completion under FHA supervision applicable to proposed construction.

5. By contracting to sell property, as proposed construction or existing construction not previously occupied, to a veteran purchaser who is to be assisted in the purchase by a loan made, guaranteed, or insured by VA, the builder or other seller agrees to place any downpayment received by the seller or agent of the seller in a special trust account as required by section 3706 of title 38, U.S. Code.

6. The VA guaranty is subject to and conditioned upon the lending institution's compliance, at the time of the making, increasing, extending or renewing of the proposed loan, with section 102 of P.L. 93-234, "Flood Disaster Protection Act of 1973."

12. PURCHASER'S NAME AND ADDRESS (Complete mailing address, include ZIP Code)	13. EXCEPTIONS TO GENERAL CONDITION NO. 3 ABOVE
	☐ ENERGY EFFICIENT MORTGAGE PROGRAM - The buyer may wish to contact a qualified person/firm for a home energy audit to identify needed energy efficiency improvements to the property. In some localities, the utility company may perform this service. The mortgage amount may be increased as a result of making energy efficiency improvements such as: Solar or conventional heating/cooling systems, water heaters, insulation, weather-stripping/caulking, and storm windows/doors. Other energy related improvements may also be considered. The mortgage may be increased by (a) up to $3,000 based solely on documented costs; or, (b) up to $6,000 provided the increase in monthly mortgage payment does not exceed the likely reduction in monthly utility costs; or, (c) more than $6000 subject to a value determination by VA.
	☐ OTHER (Cite and explain in Item 26 below)

SPECIFIC CONDITIONS (Applicable when checked or completed)

14. THE REASONABLE VALUE ESTABLISHED HEREIN FOR THE RELATED PROPERTY IS:	15. PROPOSED CONSTRUCTION TO BE COMPLETED
☐ BASED UPON OBSERVATION OF THE PROPERTY IN ITS "AS IS" CONDITION ☐ PREDICATED UPON COMPLETION OF PROPOSED CONSTRUCTION (If checked, complete Item 15) ☐ PREDICATED UPON COMPLETION OF REPAIRS LISTED IN ITEM 17	

16. INSPECTIONS REQUIRED	17. REPAIRS TO BE COMPLETED
☐ FHA COMPLIANCE INSPECTIONS FOR PROPOSED CONSTRUCTION ☐ VA COMPLIANCE INSPECTIONS ☐ LENDER TO CERTIFY	

18. NAME OF COMPLIANCE INSPECTOR	

19. HEALTH AUTHORITY APPROVAL - Execution of Health Authority form or letter indicating approval of the individual: ☐ WATER SUPPLY ☐ SEWAGE DISPOSAL SYSTEM	20. ☐ This document is subject to the provisions of Executive Orders 11246 and 11375, and the Rules and Regulations of the Secretary of Labor in effect on this date, and 38 CFR 36.4390 through 36.4393, and also the provisions of the certification executed by the builder, sponsor or developer named herein which is on file in this office.

21. ☐ WOOD DESTROYING INSECT INFORMATION - EXISTING CONSTRUCTION - The seller shall, at no cost to the veteran-purchaser, prior to settlement, obtain a written statement from a qualified pest control operator reporting wood destroying insect information using the NPCA-1, National Pest Control Association form or other form acceptable to VA.

22. WARRANTY ☐ (If checked, complete Item 23)	23. NAME OF WARRANTOR	24. ☐ Since this property is located in a Special Flood Hazard Area as established by FEMA, flood insurance will be required in accordance with 38 CFR 36.4326

25. SAFE DRINKING WATER ACT
☐ Certification required that in construction, any solders and flux did not contain more than 0.2 percent lead and any pipes and pipe fittings did not contain more than 8.0 percent lead.

26. OTHER REQUIREMENTS

OMB APPROVED NO. 2900-0045
RESPONDENT BURDEN: 12 minutes

CERTIFICATE OF REASONABLE VALUE

1. CASE NUMBER		4. TITLE LIMITATIONS AND RESTRICTIVE COVENANTS:
2. PROPERTY ADDRESS (Include ZIP Code and county)	3. LEGAL DESCRIPTION	

1. ☐ CONDOMINIUM   2. ☐ PLANNED UNIT DEVELOPMENT

5. NAME AND ADDRESS OF FIRM OR PERSON MAKING REQUEST/APPLICATION (Include ZIP Code)	6. REMAINING ECONOMIC LIFE OF PROPERTY IS ESTIMATED TO BE NOT LESS THAN (Enter number of years)

YEARS

7. ESTIMATED REASONABLE VALUE OF PROPERTY	8. EXPIRATION DATE
$	

9. SECRETARY OF VETERANS AFFAIRS BY (Signature of authorized agent)

10. DATE ISSUED	11. VA OFFICE

GENERAL CONDITIONS

(NOTE: THE DEPARTMENT OF VETERANS AFFAIRS DOES NOT ASSUME ANY RESPONSIBILITY FOR THE CONDITION OF THE PROPERTY. THE CORRECTION OF ANY DEFECTS NOW EXISTING OR THAT MAY DEVELOP WILL BE THE RESPONSIBILITY OF THE PURCHASER.)

1. This certificate will remain effective as to any written contract of sale entered into by an eligible veteran within the validity period indicated.
2. This dwelling conforms with the Minimum Property Requirements prescribed by the Secretary of Veterans Affairs.
3. The aggregate of any loan secured by this property plus the amount of any assessment consequent on any special improvements as to which a lien or right to a lien shall exist against the property, except as provided in Item 13 below, may not exceed the reasonable value in Item 7 above.
4. Proposed construction shall be completed in accordance with the plans and specifications identified below, relating to both onsite and offsite improvements upon which this valuation is based and shall otherwise conform fully to the VA Minimum Property Requirements. Satisfactory completion must be evidenced by either:
   A. VA Final Compliance Inspection Report (VA Form 26-1839), or
   B. VA Acceptance of FHA Compliance Inspection Reports or other evidence of completion under FHA supervision applicable to proposed construction.
5. By contracting to sell property, as proposed construction or existing construction not previously occupied, to a veteran purchaser who is to be assisted in the purchase by a loan made, guaranteed, or insured by VA, the builder or other seller agrees to place any downpayment received by the seller or agent of the seller in a special trust account as required by section 3706 of title 38, U.S. Code.
6. The VA guaranty is subject to and conditioned upon the lending institution's compliance, at the time of the making, increasing, extending or renewing of the proposed loan, with section 102 of P.L. 93-234, "Flood Disaster Protection Act of 1973."

12. PURCHASER'S NAME AND ADDRESS (Complete mailing address, Include ZIP Code)	13. EXCEPTIONS TO GENERAL CONDITION NO. 3 ABOVE
	☐ ENERGY EFFICIENT MORTGAGE PROGRAM - The buyer may wish to contact a qualified person/firm for a home energy audit to identify needed energy efficiency improvements to the property. In some localities, the utility company may perform this service. The mortgage amount may be increased as a result of making energy efficiency improvements such as: Solar or conventional heating/cooling systems, water heaters, insulation, weather-stripping/caulking, and storm windows/doors. Other energy related improvements may also be considered. The mortgage may be increased by (a) up to $3,000 based solely on documented costs; or, (b) up to $6,000 provided the increase in monthly mortgage payment does not exceed the likely reduction in monthly utility costs, or, (c) more than $6000 subject to a value determination by VA. ☐ OTHER (Cite and explain in Item 26 below)

SPECIFIC CONDITIONS (Applicable when checked or completed)

14. THE REASONABLE VALUE ESTABLISHED HEREIN FOR THE RELATED PROPERTY IS:	15. PROPOSED CONSTRUCTION TO BE COMPLETED
☐ BASED UPON OBSERVATION OF THE PROPERTY IN ITS "AS IS" CONDITION ☐ PREDICATED UPON COMPLETION OF PROPOSED CONSTRUCTION (If checked, complete Item 15) ☐ PREDICATED UPON COMPLETION OF REPAIRS LISTED IN ITEM 17	

16. INSPECTIONS REQUIRED	17. REPAIRS TO BE COMPLETED
☐ FHA COMPLIANCE INSPECTIONS FOR PROPOSED CONSTRUCTION ☐ VA COMPLIANCE INSPECITONS ☐ LENDER TO CERTIFY	

18. NAME OF COMPLIANCE INSPECTOR

19. HEALTH AUTHORITY APPROVAL - Execution of Health Authority form or letter indicating approval of the individual:	20.
☐ WATER SUPPLY ☐ SEWAGE DISPOSAL SYSTEM	☐ This document is subject to the provisions of Executive Orders 11246 and 11375, and the Rules and Regulations of the Secretary of Labor in effect on this date, and 38 CFR 36.4390 through 36.4393, and also the provisions of the certification executed by the builder, sponsor or developer named herein which is on file in this office.

21. ☐ WOOD DESTROYING INSECT INFORMATION - EXISTING CONSTRUCTION - The seller shall, at no cost to the veteran-purchaser, prior to settlement, obtain a written statement from a qualified pest control operator reporting wood destroying insect information using the NPCA-1, National Pest Control Association form or other form acceptable to VA.

22. WARRANTY ☐ (If checked, complete Item 23)	23. NAME OF WARRANTOR	24. ☐ Since this property is located in a Special Flood Hazard Area as established by FEMA, flood insurance will be required in accordance with 38 CFR 36.4326

25. SAFE DRINKING WATER ACT
☐ Certification required that in construction, any solders and flux did not contain more than 0.2 percent lead and any pipes and pipe fittings did not contain more than 8.0 percent lead.

26. OTHER REQUIREMENTS

VA FORM JUN 2001   **26-1843**   SUPERSEDES VA FORM 26-1805, DEC 1992, WHICH WILL NOT BE USED.   **PURCHASER'S COPY 5**

OMB APPROVED NO. 2900-0045
RESPONDENT BURDEN: 12 minutes

REQUEST FOR DETERMINATION OF REASONABLE VALUE (Real Estate)

1. CASE NUMBER		4. TITLE LIMITATIONS AND RESTRICTIVE COVENANTS:
2. PROPERTY ADDRESS (Include ZIP Code and county)	3. LEGAL DESCRIPTION	

1. ☐ CONDOMINIUM   2. ☐ PLANNED UNIT DEVELOPMENT

5. NAME AND ADDRESS OF FIRM OR PERSON MAKING REQUEST/APPLICATION (Include ZIP Code)

6. LOT DIMENSIONS:

1. ☐ IRREGULAR: SQ/FT   2. ☐ ACRES:

7. UTILITIES (✓)	ELEC.	GAS	WATER	SAN. SEWER
1. PUBLIC				
2. COMMUNITY				
3. INDIVIDUAL				

8. EQUIP.
1. ☐ RANGE/OVEN   4. ☐ CLOTHES WASHER   7. ☐ VENT FAN
2. ☐ REFRIG.   5. ☐ DRYER   8. ☐ W/W CARPET
3. ☐ DISH WASHER   6. ☐ GARBAGE DISPOSAL   9. ☐

9. BUILDING STATUS	3. ☐ EXISTING	10. BUILDING TYPE	11. FACTORY FABRICATED?	12A. NO. OF BUILDINGS	12B. NO. OF LIVING UNITS	13A. STREET ACCESS	13B. STREET MAINTENANCE
1. ☐ PROPOSED	ALTERATIONS, IMPROVEMENTS.	1. ☐ DETACHED 3. ☐ ROW				1. ☐ PRIVATE	1. ☐ PRIVATE
2. ☐ UNDER CONSTRUCTION 4. ☐ OR REPAIRS		2. ☐ SEMI-DETACHED 4. ☐ APT. UNIT	1. ☐ YES 2. ☐ NO			2. ☐ PUBLIC	2. ☐ PUBLIC

14A. CONSTRUCTION WARRANTY INCLUDED?	14B. NAME OF WARRANTY PROGRAM	14C. EXPIRATION DATE (Month, day, year)	15. CONSTRUCTION COMPLETED (Mo.,yr.)
1. ☐ YES 2. ☐ NO (If "Yes," complete Items 14b and 14c also)			

16. NAME OF OWNER	17. PROPERTY:	18. RENT (If applic.)
	☐ OCCUPIED BY OWNER ☐ NEVER OCCUPIED ☐ VACANT ☐ OCCUPIED BY TENANT (Complete Item 18 also)	$ / MONTH

19. NAME OF OCCUPANT	20. TELEPHONE NO.	21. NAME OF BROKER	22. TELEPHONE NO.	23. DATE AND TIME AVAILABLE FOR INSPECTION ☐ AM ☐ PM
24. KEYS AT (Address)		25. ORIGINATOR'S IDENT. NO.	26. SPONSOR'S IDENT. NO.	27. INSTITUTION'S CASE NO.

28. PURCHASER'S NAME AND ADDRESS (Complete mailing address, Include ZIP Code)

EQUAL OPPORTUNITY IN HOUSING
NOTE: Federal laws and regulations prohibit discrimination because of race, color, religion, sex, or national origin in the sale or rental of residential property. Numerous State statutes and local ordinances also prohibit such discrimination. In addition, section 805 of the Civil Rights Act of 1968 prohibits discriminatory practices in connection with the financing of housing.

If VA finds there is noncompliance with any antidiscrimination laws or regulations, it may discontinue business with the violator.

29. NEW OR PROPOSED CONSTRUCTION - Complete Items 29A through 29G for new or proposed construction cases only

A. COMPLIANCE INSPECTIONS WILL BE OR WERE MADE BY:	B. PLANS (Check one)	C. PLANS SUBMITTED PREVIOUSLY UNDER CASE NO.
☐ FHA ☐ VA ☐ NONE MADE	☐ FIRST SUBMISSION ☐ REPEAT CASE (If checked complete Item 29C)	
D. NAME AND ADDRESS OF BUILDER	E. TELEPHONE NO. F. NAME AND ADDRESS OF WARRANTOR	G. TELEPHONE NO.

30. COMMENTS ON SPECIAL ASSESSMENTS OR HOMEOWNERS ASSOCIATION CHARGES	31. ANNUAL REAL ESTATE TAXES $	33. LEASEHOLD CASES (Complete if applicable)
	32. MINERAL RIGHTS RESERVED? ☐ YES (Explain) ☐ NO	A. LEASE IS: ☐ 99 YEARS ☐ RENEWABLE B. EXPIRES (Date) C. ANNUAL GROUND RENT $

34A. SALE PRICE OF PROPERTY	34B. IS BUYER PURCHASING LOT SEPARATELY?	35. REFINANCING-AMOUNT OF PROPOSED LOAN	36. PROPOSED SALE CONTRACT ATTACHED	37. CONTRACT NO. PREVIOUSLY APPROVED BY VA THAT WILL BE
$	(If "Yes," see instruction page under "Sale Price") ☐ YES ☐ NO	$	☐ YES ☐ NO	

38. REMARKS

ASSIGNMENT OF APPRAISER

39. DATE OF ASSIGNMENT	40. SIGNATURE OF LOAN GUARANTY OFFICER OR DESIGNEE	NOTE TO APPRAISER: You are assigned to make an appraisal of the above-described property and to submit your report to this office. If Item 1, 3 or 4 of block 9 is checked, you must submit two copies of the report. Your estimate of reasonable value is subject to administrative adjustment. If existing construction is appraised, you must gain access to the interior of the property to be appraised, and two photos (different views) of the subject property must be submitted with your report. A front-view picture of each comparable used in the market data analysis must also be provided with your report unless this appraisal involves a low-rise or high-rise condominium, or a horizontal condominium development or townhouse planned-unit development, provided the comparables are located in the same project as the subject property and are considered substantially identical to the subject property in design (i.e., same unit type constructed by same builder). If you cannot complete this assignment in 5 days, please notify the Loan Guaranty Officer or designee immediately.
41. NAME AND ADDRESS OF APPRAISER (Complete mailing address, Include ZIP Code)		

*Photos of the subject property are required only if Item 3 or 4 is checked.

VA FORM JUN 2001   **26-1805   APPRAISER'S COPY 6**

OMB Approved No. 2900-0086
Respondent Burden: 15 minutes

REQUEST FOR A CERTIFICATE OF ELIGIBILITY		**TO**	Department of Veterans Affairs Attn: Loan Guaranty Division

NOTE: Please read information on reverse before completing this form. If additional space is required, attach a separate she

1. FIRST-MIDDLE-LAST NAME OF VETERAN	2. DATE OF BIRTH	3. VETERAN'S DAYTIME TELEPHONE NO. (_ _)

4. ADDRESS OF VETERAN (No., street or rural route, city or P.O., State and ZIP Code)	5. MAIL CERTIFICATE OF ELIGIBILITY TO: (Complete ONLY if the Certificate is to be mailed to an address different from the one listed in Item 4)

6. MILITARY SERVICE DATA (ATTACH PROOF OF SERVICE - SEE PARAGRAPH "D" ON REVERSE)

A. ITEM	B. PERIODS OF ACTIVE SERVICE		C. NAME (Show your name exactly as it appears on your separation papers or Statement of Service)	D. SOCIAL SECURITY NUMBER	E. SERVICE NUMBER (If different from Social Security No.)	F. BRANCH SERVIC
	DATE FROM	DATE TO				
1.						
2.						
3.						
4.						

7A. WERE YOU DISCHARGED, RETIRED OR SEPARATED FROM SERVICE BECAUSE OF DISABILITY OR DO YOU NOW HAVE ANY SERVICE-CONNECTED DISABILITIES? ☐ YES ☐ NO (If "Yes," complete Item 7B)	7B. VA CLAIM FILE NUMBER C-

8. PREVIOUS VA LOANS (Must answer N/A if no previous VA home loan. DO NOT LEAVE BLANK)

A. ITEM	B. TYPE (Home, Refinance, Manufactured Home, or Direct)	C. ADDRESS OF PROPERTY	D. DATE OF LOAN	E. DO YOU STILL OWN THE PROPERTY? (YES/NO)	F. DATE PROPERTY WAS SOLD (Submit a copy of HUD-1, Settlement Statement, if available)	G. VA LOAN NUM (If known)
1.						
2.						
3.						
4.						
5.						
6.						

I CERTIFY THAT the statements herein are true to the best of my knowledge and belief.

9. SIGNATURE OF VETERAN (Do NOT print)	10. DATE SIGNED

FEDERAL STATUTES PROVIDE SEVERE PENALTIES FOR FRAUD, INTENTIONAL MISREPRESENTATION, CRIMINAL CONNIVANCE OR CONSPIRACY PURPOSED TO INFLUENCE THE ISSUANCE OF ANY GUARANTY OR INSURANCE BY THE SECRETARY OF VETERANS AFFAI

FOR VA USE ONLY

11A. DATE CERTIFICATE ISSUED	11B. SIGNATURE OF VA AGENT

VA FORM **26-1880**
FEB 2000

SUPERSEDES VA FORM 26-1880, MAR 1999,
WHICH WILL NOT BE USED.

INSTRUCTIONS FOR VA FORM 26-1880

.CY ACT INFORMATION: No Certificate of Eligibility may be issued unless VA receives sufficient information to determine that you are eligible (38 3702). You are not required to furnish the information, including the Social Security Number, but are urged to do so, since it is vital to proper action by your case. Specifically, your Social Security Number is requested under authority of 38 U.S.C. 3702 and is requested only if the service department used ocial Security Number as a service number. Failure to provide a completed application will deprive VA of information needed in reaching decisions could affect you. Responses may be disclosed outside VA only if the disclosure is authorized under the Privacy Act, including the routine uses identified VA system of records, 55VA26, Loan Guaranty Home, Condominium and Manufactured Home Loan Applicant Records, Specially Adapted Housing ant Records, and Vendee Loan Applicant Records - VA, published in the Federal Register.

●NDENT BURDEN: VA may not conduct or sponsor, and respondent is not required to respond to this collection of information unless it displays a ●MB Control Number. Public reporting burden for this collection of information is estimated to average 15 minutes per response, including the time for ng instructions, searching existing data sources, gathering and maintaining the data needed, and completing and reviewing the collection of information. have comments regarding this burden estimate or any other aspect of this collection of information, call 1-800-827-1000 for mailing information on where your comments.

il this completed form, along with proof of service, to the Eligibility Center at P.O. Box 20729, Winston-Salem, NC 27120 (for veterans located in stern half of the country) or P.O. Box 240097, Los Angeles, CA 90024 (for veterans located in the western half of the country). Veterans ed overseas may use either address.

itary Service Requirements for VA Loan Eligibility: (NOTE: Cases involving other than honorable discharges will usually require further pment by VA. This is necessary to determine if the service was under other than dishonorable conditions.)

artime Service. If you served anytime during World War II (September 16, 1940 to July 25, 1947), Korean Conflict (June 27, 1950 to January 31, or Vietnam Era (August 5, 1964 to May 7, 1975) you must have served at least 90 days on active duty and have been discharged or released under other shonorable conditions. If you served less than 90 days, you may be eligible if discharged because of service-connected disability.

acetime Service. If your service fell entirely within one of the following periods: July 26, 1947 to June 26, 1950, or February 1, 1955 to August 4, 1964, ıst have served at least 181 days of continuous active duty and have been discharged or released under conditions other than dishonorable. If you entered after May 7, 1975 but prior to September 8, 1980 (enlisted) or October 17, 1981 (officer) and completed your service before August 2, 1990, 181 days is also required. If you served less than 181 days, you may be eligible if discharged for a service-connected disability.

ırvice after September 7, 1980 (enlisted) or October 16, 1981 (officer) and prior to August 2, 1990. If you were separated from service which began ese dates, you must have: (a) Completed 24 months of continuous active duty for the full period (at least 181 days) for which you were called or ordered e duty, and been discharged or released under conditions other than dishonorable; or (b) Completed at least 181 days of active duty and been discharged he specific authority of 10 U.S.C. 1173 (hardship discharge) or 10 U.S.C. 1171 (early out discharge), or have been determined to have a compensable -connected disability; or (c) Been discharged with less than 181 days of service for a service-connected disability. Individuals may also be eligible if they released from active duty due to an involuntary reduction in force, certain medical conditions, or, in some instances, for the convenience of the ıment.

ılf War. If you served on active duty during the Gulf War (August 2, 1990 to a date yet to be determined), you must have: (a) Completed 24 months of ıous active duty or the full period (at least 90 days) for which you were called or ordered to active duty, and been discharged or released under conditions han dishonorable; or (b) Completed at least 90 days of active duty and been discharged under the specific authority of 10 U.S.C. 1173 (hardship ge), or 10 U.S.C. 1171 (early out discharge), or have been determined to have a compensable service-connected disability; or (c) Been discharged with ın 90 days of service for a service-connected disability. Individuals may also be eligible if they were released from active duty due to an involuntary ion in force, certain medical conditions, or, in some instances, for the convenience of the Government.

tive Duty Service Personnel. If you are now on active duty, you are eligible after having served on continuous active duty for at least 181 days (90 days the Persian Gulf War) unless discharged or separated from a previous qualifying period of active duty service.

ılected Reserve Requirements for VA Loan Eligibility. If you are not otherwise eligible and you have completed a total of 6 years in the Selected ıes or National Guard (member of an active unit, attended required weekend drills and 2-week active duty training) and (a) Were discharged with an ıble discharge; or (b) Were placed on the retired list or (c) Were transferred to the Standby Reserve or an element of the Ready Reserve other than the ı Reserve after Service characterized as honorable service; or (d) Continue to serve in the Selected Reserve. Individuals who completed less than 6 years ı eligible if discharged for a service-connected disability. Eligibility for Selected Reservists expires September 30, 2007.

married surviving spouses of eligible veterans seeking determination of basic eligibility for VA Loan Guaranty benefits are NOT required to ı te this form, but are required to complete VA Form 26-1817, Request for Determination of Loan Guaranty Eligibility-Unmarried Surviving e.

ıof of Military Service

ıRegular" Veterans. Attach to this request your most recent discharge or separation papers from active military duty since September 16, 1940, which ıctive duty dates and type of discharge. If you were separated after January 1, 1950, DD Form 214 must be submitted. If you were separated after October ı, and you received DD Form 214, Certificate of Release or Discharge From Active Duty, 1 July edition, VA must be furnished Copy 4 of the form. ıay submit either original papers or legible copies. In addition, if you are now on active duty submit a statement of service signed by, or by direction of, ıutant, personnel officer, or commander of your unit or higher headquarters showing date of entry on your current active duty period and the duration of ıne lost. Any Veterans Services Representative in the nearest Department of Veterans Affairs office or center will assist you in securing necessary proof of ıy service.

ılected Reserves/National Guard. If you are a discharged member of the Army or Air Force National Guard you may submit a NGB Form 22, Report of ıtion and Record of Service, or NGB Form 23, Retirement Points Accounting, or it's equivalent (this is similar to a retirement points summary). If you are ıarged member of the Selected Reserve you may submit a copy of your latest annual point statement and evidence of honorable service. You may submit ıyour original papers or legible copies. Since there is no single form used by the Reserves or National Guard similar to the DD Form 214, it is your ısibility to furnish adequate documentation of at least 6 years of honorable service. In addition, if you are currently serving in the Selected Reserve you ıubmit a statement of service signed by, or by the direction of, the adjutant, personnel officer or commander of your unit or higher headquarters showing ıgth of time that you have been a member of the unit.

Index

About the Author

Ms. Diana Brodman Summers received her J.D. from Depaul University College of Law and her undergraduate degree from Roosevelt University. She is an arbitrator for both Cook and DuPage Counties' mandatory arbitration programs and was recently appointed to the Liquor Commission for the City of Downers Grove. Ms. Summers is an active member of the Association of Trial Lawyers of America, the American Bar Association, the DuPage County Bar Association, and the Illinois State Bar Association.

Ms. Summers has taught seminars for lawyers through several bar associations and has written articles on computerizing law offices. She currently volunteers with other Illinois State Bar Association attorneys in accordance with the local Judge Advocate General's office to provide low-cost legal service for returning members of the military. She currently maintains a law practice in Lisle, Illinois, a suburb of Chicago.